WILDLY PROFITABLE MARKETING
for the Pet Industry

Praise for
Wildly Profitable Marketing for the Pet Industry

"*Wildly Profitable Marketing* is wildly wonderful! Pam Foster and C S Wurzberger have put together all the ingredients to create and implement a wildly successful marketing strategy for your business. The checklists alone are worth the price of this outstanding book.

No matter where you are in your pet business, this book will become your go-to resource for marketing help. Dive in now so you can benefit immediately — because it's true, if people don't know about you, they can't buy from you."

— Shawna Schuh, Women in the Pet Industry

"*Wildly Profitable Marketing for the Pet Industry* is a must-have for today's veterinarian who wants to remain competitive in an ever-increasingly digital savvy and marketing sensitive industry. The pressures on practices today to stay on top of an array of technologies normally outside their expertise can be overwhelming.

Pam and C S have managed to effectively convey a large amount of information into 14 concise chapters crafted specifically for the pet industry professional. This book will be a great resource as veterinarians and practice managers look for new strategies to drive revenue through increased clinic visits and compliance rates."

— Stewart Wright, Product and Marketing Manager,
LifeLearn/WebDVM4

"As small-company owners, we can't say enough about this book regarding the importance of website content plus the use of postcards and letters. We hired Pam to revise and correctly SEO our website (which was woefully in need of help) and to assist us in writing a powerful letter and postcard. The suggestions in this book will give you the ability to bring in success beyond your dreams."

— Jeanne Wolfington and Krystal Hanson, PuppyStairs.com

Wildly Profitable Marketing for the Pet Industry

Powerful pointers for your pet
business, veterinary practice
or pet-industry supply company

Pam Foster and C S Wurzberger

From the Pawzoola Publishing.com Library

ISBN 978-0615632940

Cover design by Bonnie Carberry
Interior design by Michael Steere

Wildly Profitable Marketing for the Pet Industry
From the Pawzoola Publishing.com library
a division of aTriptotheZoo.com
P.O. Box 1779
Wilmington, VT 05363
www.PawzoolaPublishing.com

DISCLAIMER

This book/workbook is designed to provide information on creating a Profit Producing Planner through the suggested steps and guidelines that include up-front planning, hiring a great team, marketing tactics and measuring the results. It is sold with the understanding that the publishers and the authors are not engaged in rendering legal, accounting or other professional services not of a marketing nature. If legal or other such expert assistance is required, the services of a competent professional in that field should be sought.

It is not the purpose of this workbook to reprint all the information otherwise available throughout the Internet and marketing community, but instead to compile, curate, complement, amplify and supplement the highlights of that information. You are urged to read other materials that can provide more detail or other opinions about marketing and tailor the information to your individual needs.

Anyone who decides to create a profitable marketing plan must expect to invest time, effort and money into it. While we can and do feature tips that have brought successful results to many businesses, we cannot guarantee or even promise that every business can use these tips to gain profits. Other factors beyond our control, including a business's structure, products, pricing, marketing efforts, target audience and follow-through, will affect the performance of a website or plan.

Contents

PART THREE   134

Cultivate profitable relationships using today's
best marketing tools.

This is the heart of your marketing… where you'll create a brilliant
strategy including popular methods that work wonders today:

8

Foreword

By James Carroll
Chief Operating Officer
LifeLearn, Inc.
Guelph, Ontario, Canada

Marketing a business with impact has always required a certain amount of education, experience, character and business sense, sprinkled with a little luck now and again. But in today's world, new avenues available to marketers are evolving at light speed, creating the additional challenge of simply keeping up with the technology.

It used to be that the most successful companies were the ones that had substantial advertising and marketing budgets, investing in creative television and magazine ads to grab our attention. However, with the surge of social media, we now see small organizations with similarly small budgets reaching their target audiences using tools such as Facebook, Twitter, YouTube, LinkedIn and a myriad of other ever-evolving online communities. And because social media, blogging and search engine optimization have become an integral part of our lives as consumers, we must incorporate online marketing strategies into our businesses in order to thrive.

For example, I was recently visiting one of our partner organizations in Scotland, and over a dinner conversation learned that they were in the process of hiring a "Community Manager." I had not heard this term before, but quickly learned that this role is entirely focused on their social media strategy and execution. By creating engagement with online communities, our partner is in essence driving loyalty and referrals while replacing some of the more traditional and costly direct-to-consumer marketing tactics.

This is not to say that every small business needs to invest in a team dedicated only to social media, but it does show the trend of increasing importance that online strategies play for marketers globally.

The pet industry is a particularly unique and interesting business, but certainly not exempt from the challenges of reaching consumers and clients. Pet owners are highly engaged when it comes to their furry family members, as can be witnessed by the endless number of images, videos and postings dedicated to animals. According to the 2008 U.S. Pet Ownership and Demographic Sourcebook, there are 72.1 million dogs and 81.7 million cats living in homes across the United States.

Needless to say, whether you're an individual selling lifestyle products such as beds and collars, or services such as grooming, boarding or veterinary care, pet owners are looking for you online. Similarly, if you're a supplier to the pet and/or veterinary industry, potential clients are on the search for your products. And, they're most frequently looking online as well.

Wildly Profitable Marketing for the Pet Industry is an outstanding new resource for those of us that understand the need to incorporate dynamic marketing strategies into our businesses.

From the basics of defining your mission and understanding your competition, to more advanced tactics including tools such as social media, email and search engine optimization to create an engaging online presence, Pam Foster and C S Wurzberger outline the steps that will help your organization achieve results.

The principles in the chapters that follow are dedicated to creating clarity and customer focus within your business, helping you to position your products or services, create a powerful brand presence, and set your business apart. Having worked with Pam for many years, I have enjoyed benefiting from her enthusiasm and expertise, most recently with her work on MyPetED.com.

Having built my career for nearly 20 years in this space, I am personally excited to see a marketing guide written specifically for the pet and veterinary industries. *Wildly Profitable Marketing for the Pet Industry* provides a solid foundation where the latest practices can be applied to the world of marketing to pet professionals and veterinary practices in this very unique and ever-changing industry.

By using this guide and applying the strategies within, you will have started down the path for success.

Acknowledgments

We'd like to thank a number of people who have personally supported us in creating this guide.

Pam would like to dedicate this book to Jillian, Ben, Lee, Andy, Carolyn, Billy, Sue and her entire family for always encouraging her to follow her passion. Pam would also like to thank prolific how-to author Bob Bly for his unending generosity and his personal review and "thumbs up" of our previous marketing books under the Internet Jungle Guide brand; the foundation of this guide. She'd also like to thank her copywriter colleagues who edited previous versions of this book: Eddie Adelman, Lee Schwarz and Laura Armbruster. In addition, Pam would like to acknowledge the wonderful supporting role of pets she's known all her life, including those who share her life now: Louie and Jack.

C S would like to dedicate this book to her daughter Emily who continues to inspire and push her to be all she is meant to be, and her twin grandson's Landon and Colton who bring such joy to her and drive her to help save endangered animals of the world so they will be around for them and future generations. To her soul sister Susan who continues to remind her of the importance of walking lightly on the earth. To Jack Hanna and Jane Goodall who put the passion in her heart and paved the way for her to create her dream career teaching people to care and respect animals. And finally to the Dodo bird for giving her a lifetime of passion to propel her forward . . . and to all the animals that have entered her life through the years, reminding her that unconditional love is the best part of life.

We'd both like to thank the inspiring clients, marketing professionals, and pet industry colleagues who we've had the honor to work with, including:

- Shawna Schuh, Women in the Pet Industry
- Mike Linville of Black Dog Studios, partner at PetIndustryTV.com
- Our book designer Mike Steere
- Our proofreader Nan Hughes
- Joseph Pagano, Immediatag, LLC
- EmilySusan007.com
- Chris Kelly, Kirk Augustine and Rick Boggess, *Veterinary Advantage* magazine
- The following pet businesses and veterinary companies:

A Trip to the Zoo.com
Animal Emergency Clinic
Ben's Bark Ave. Bistro
BioVision Technologies
BRL Sciences: EPO-Equine
Cornerstone Practice Management Systems
DirectVet Marketing
Dog-On-It Parks
Downtown Hound Doggie Lounge
IDEXX Laboratories
LifeLearn
LL Bean Dog Products
Luckydog Day & Night Care
MyPetED.com
NK Dog Walking.com
Osspet
Pawsitive Perks
PetAmberAlert.com
Pet Health Network

Puppy Stairs Original Pet Ramps and Steps
Radiopet
St. Francis Pet Medals and Pet ID Tags
ZooMarketingTools.com

We appreciate and acknowledge the marketing pioneers and guides who tirelessly test today's marketing platforms and teach us about what's working. We humbly thank them for their leadership in the marketing field, and in some cases, their personal mentorship. They include:

* Heather Lloyd-Martin, SuccessWorks
* Chris Kelly, Veterinary Advantage
* Seth Godin
* Chris Brogan
* MarketingExperiments.com
* David Meerman Scott
* Brendan Burchard
* Tony Robbins

Finally, we thank you for choosing this book.

We know you have countless marketing resources available to you. We're proud and thrilled to finally offer you a guide that's specific for pet industry professionals and your mission within that world. We wish you great success with your marketing!

Introduction

At last: a hands-on marketing field guide designed specifically for the pet industry!

This includes pet retailers, pet product companies, pet groomers, doggie daycares, dog walkers, pet sitters and trainers, pet shelters, veterinary practices, equine businesses and other pet-related businesses, including suppliers/vendors to this industry.

To maintain clarity in this guide and help you focus on the marketing principles you'll discover, we use the term pet businesses quite a bit, but we're referring to all pet and veterinary-industry organizations and their vendors/suppliers.

Dear Marketing Professional:

Pet ownership and pet-care spending is at an all-time high in many categories, and that's great news for you.

* According to the American Pet Products Association (APPA)'s 2013-2014 National Pet Owners Survey, 68% of U.S. households own a pet, which equates to 82.5 million homes.

* For 2013, an estimated $55.53 billion will be spent on our pets in the U.S. alone, in the areas of food and treats, supplies and over-the-

counter medicines, veterinary care, live animal purchases and pet services, such as grooming and boarding. (APPA data)

* And in the 2013-2014 APPA survey, basic annual expenses for dog and cat owners in dollars included these numbers (APPA data):

	Dogs	Cats
Surgical Vet Visits	$621	$382
Routine Vet	$231	$193
Food	$239	$203
Food Treats	$65	$36
Kennel Boarding	$327	$337
Vitamins	$64	$77
Travel Expenses	$78	$48
Groomer/Grooming Aids	$61	$20
Toys	$41	$23

These are just the basic numbers. You probably spend much more than this each year on your own pets' care, just like we do.

So, with these trends, it's a great time to be in the pet industry! Right? Well, yes, if your marketing is solid and getting a great return on your marketing investment.

But, it's not all about money. We know you probably didn't get into the pet industry just to make big bucks.

We also know that most pet-professionals and veterinary practice marketers work like dogs, putting in long hours and juggling mindboggling priorities on a daily basis... with the mission of serving the pet industry while making a good living.

We know all kinds of wonderful, dedicated pet fans who have followed their passion to run a pet business or veterinary practice . . . and who are thriving yet feeling overwhelmed with their many roles.

Each of these pet-lovers turned pet professionals have their own stories about the day they realized it was time to build a business based on pet care, or fun pet products, or brilliant solutions for those who work with pets.

Perhaps these stories sound familiar.

- Brad was a state trooper responsible for K-9 dog training and care. When he retired, he opened a natural pet food store dedicated to helping pet parents learn about the best foods for their pets' lasting health. He's become one of the state's authorities on organic, safe pet food.

- Dr. Fred has been a forward-thinking veterinarian for his entire career, and he is dedicated to having the best equipment, staff and communications methods so he can serve his clients with excellent pet care. Through his commitment, his practice is thriving in a time when many are not.

- Jeanne had a 5-pound Yorkshire terrier who became disabled and required neurosurgery. After his surgery, she searched for steps to enable him to get up and down from the couch and bed. She couldn't find anything that was high-quality construction or complementary to her décor, so she and a friend invented a solution and launched a pet ramps and steps business.

- Mandie had a beloved rescue dog named Lucky, who inspired her to open a world-class doggie daycare in her hometown. Her thriving center is the best game in town, and she's expanded to a second location in another state.

- The inventor of the Water Walker Leash noticed how a pleasant walk with his best friend was turning into a task. When he began to notice others on their walks, it was confirmed. Everyone had the same problem, struggling with a dog water bottle, a water bowl, wastebags, snacks — plus the dog leash. A light came on, and the retractable Water Walker Leash was conceived.

* When Kathy and Gary, a couple in the Northwest, combined her 35 years of experience as a veterinary assistant, showing and breeding dogs — with his 25 years of experience designing playground equipment for public parks — the result was, and is, a pet-friendly product designed by experts to last in any kind of tough outdoor environment after repeated use by thousands of dogs.

* The Marketing Director for a leading pet insurance company is working hard to continue strengthening the company's brand awareness, both online and in print, to boost sales. Her biggest challenge is setting the brand apart from a growing number of fierce competitors in this exploding market... as well as keeping up with today's various marketing channels including social media and mobile marketing.

* Chris, a sales executive who had worked in the human medical industry, saw an opportunity to bring his experience into the veterinary marketing world. He started a magazine specifically for sales reps working for all types of suppliers to veterinary practices. His magazine has grown steadily, and he's launched a second publication for the livestock industry.

All of these stories have one thing in common: a love of pets and a commitment to offering solutions within the pet or veterinary industry.

We share their stories. We have both been lifelong fans of pets (including dogs, cats, horses, birds) and other animals, as you'll see in our bios at the end of this book. Plus, after many years as marketing professionals, we're committed to working in the pet industry helping clients like these and many others.

But right now, this book is about you.

What's your story? Why are you in the pet or veterinary industry?

And, how can we help you thrive this year and beyond?

Together, we're dedicated to providing you with effective, easy-to-follow marketing practices so your organization can enjoy steady, sustainable growth while you enjoy more balance in your life.

So, with pet ownership and spending at an all-time high, what's the gap between pet fans and your ability to attract them?

How can you reach more people who enjoy finding great supplies, services and medical care for their dogs, cats, horses and other animals?

Or, if you're a supplier to the pet industry, how do you turn more pet-professionals into your clients?

Many marketers have told us that this gap stems from one thing.

Today's overwhelming marketing choices — particularly online — are simply becoming too cumbersome to follow.

We understand.

We know how hard it can be to create a powerful, productive action plan that actually works; that helps you identify and generate more customers for your pet-related business in person and online —

and most importantly, **attract more customers and profits without driving yourself crazy.**

And, if you're a vendor/supplier in this industry, we know you're equally challenged when trying to reach the right audiences with solutions they need.

We know this because our work with dozens and dozens of small-to-midsize pet and veterinary business owners and marketers all started with one problem: they were struggling to compete more effectively, reach more customers, and grow their revenue.

Take heart: A clever and effective strategy doesn't have to be complicated, lengthy or cumbersome. And, you don't have to become a technical web genius yourself.

Soon you'll know what you're doing, why you're doing it, what you can do yourself, and how to hire the best professionals to help you.

We're here to guide you on a marketing expedition that leads to the creation of your Profit Producing Planner — where each step brings you closer to finding more customers and bigger profits.

In each chapter, you'll see how to...

> Map out your route,
> Set your itinerary,
> Pack the right supplies for your journey,
> Embark on a smarter path to success, and
> Enjoy the additional profits.

If you're responsible for marketing a pet-related business... you'll soon be attracting more attention, fans, customers, sales, repeat sales, loyalty and more.

If you're a supplier to this industry... you'll discover ways to present your solutions more effectively so pet and veterinary professionals who need your products and services will find you and choose you!

So, let's look deeper at the three main benefits of this field guide:

- **You'll focus on what you want your marketing materials to DO... and for whom.**

  We can't stress enough the importance of knowing your key audience, because your ideal prospects are searching for the products and services you provide. The more you know what they need from you and how you can solve their needs, the more successful you'll be in attracting them.

  You'll see how today's online marketing works, and how you can easily follow the best practices for your benefit. Plus, this guide serves as a clear, constant reminder of your sales goals. It helps you remain focused on a clear strategy for reference every day, week and month.

  No more scattered approaches. No more guessing. In short, it keeps you on your course to marketing success!

- **You'll set your itinerary, timeline and expectations.**

  We created this field guide to serve as your go-to resource for easily organizing and tracking the scope, strategies, timeline and budget of each step you take.

  You can include it in your overall business planning, so you can measure its success and stop wasting dollars on marketing that doesn't work.

- **You'll know exactly what you can do yourself, and how to confidently outsource the rest.**

  As you'll discover, many of the steps in this guide can be done by you. Other tasks require a more technical approach by an outside resource. Using this guide, you'll be armed with the knowledge to communicate clearly with online marketing professionals and control the outcome of their efforts.

Without this clarity, you may end up chasing your tail with tactics that simply don't work.

The good news is, we know a lot of pet-related business professionals who have found a clear path to online marketing success.

So, what do those professionals know that most others don't?

You're about to find out.

Since this hands-on marketing field guide is written specifically for pet- and veterinary-related organizations, you'll soon discover 100% relevant insights on:

* **The #1 most powerful marketing question to ask yourself.** The answer will bring total clarity for achieving your online marketing mission and goals.

* **The 3 core attributes that make your website work wonders for your business.** Apply these attributes to your site and watch your traffic and revenue grow!

* **Social media myths and facts:** How to deliver what your audience really wants from you in Facebook, Twitter, YouTube and more… and how to avoid the big turn-offs.

* **The smart, streamlined way to mix online and offline marketing.** We'll show you how to blend the best of both worlds for great results.

* **Clear action steps you can begin today:** At last — a clear and simple way to set up and follow a brilliant marketing plan that WORKS.

And, that's just the beginning.

Soon you'll be a wiser marketing decision maker, creating your own Profit Producing Planner and taking control of your efforts and results.

So, let's begin!

How to make the most of this guide:

We recommend going through each chapter, in order, to get the full value of this information. Take your time, perhaps even just an hour a week if that's all you can spare.

You'll benefit the most if you…

* Assess your current website and marketing efforts against our guidelines and checklists (with an open, honest mindset toward improvement),

* Check out the examples we're providing as best practices to consider following,

* Embrace the lessons and consider how they apply to your current situation,

* Complete each Profit Producing Planner Worksheet in the Appendix, and

* Create a realistic, achievable foundation for your success.

When you're done exploring each step and completing the worksheets —

Your Profit Producing Planner will show you exactly how to begin steering more and more eager prospects and customers swiftly to your door.

Just imagine seeing a growing number of happy pet-lovers singing your praises and spending more money with you! That's what you can achieve, starting now.

Enjoy your marketing success!

Pam and C S
Your Friendly Pet and Vet Marketing Guides

Start with total clarity about your organization's mission and market.

What does your business or practice have in common with these turkeys?
These turkeys are strutting their stuff in full regalia to attract the lone female who happens to be strolling by. Sadly, it's hard to tell them apart, except the one on the right has some torn tail issues. So, how does the female know which one is her soul mate, or if any of them belong by her side? It's the same for your business. How do you stand apart from your competition in ways that will attract more customers and motivate them to choose YOU? That's what this section is about. (Turkey quartet photo captured by Pam Foster)

Before embarking on any journey, you need to know exactly where you're going and why.

The same is true for marketing.

This section helps you get grounded in your purpose — the main reason you picked up this book.

* You'll determine where you stand in the marketplace, right now.

* You'll identify the people who'd love to know about you.

* You'll clear away the clutter about what you're not, which is valuable as well.

Let's dive in.

Define Your Ultimate Destination

Confirm your business mission so you'll embark on a marketing journey that actually works!

Before you create your Profit Producing Planner... you'll want to start with a clear outline of your marketing objectives, who you're trying to attract, the unique solutions you offer prospects and customers and the distinct promises and benefits to feature in your marketing.

You'll want to understand exactly what you're aiming for, right?

To get there, let's begin with your overall marketing objective.

Here's the single most important question you'll consider in this entire guide:

What do you want your marketing to DO for your organization?

We're talking about specific goals now — not just "make money." To know if your marketing efforts are successful or not, you need to identify specific, measurable sales objectives or targets, such as:

- "Generate 25,000 more website visitors this year."
- Or, "Increase your product sales by 12% this year."
- Or even, "Introduce a new product or service that generates $100,000 in revenue this year."

Why is this question so critical? Because once you clearly define your marketing objectives, you and everyone in your management and marketing-related functions, plus any marketing professionals and vendors helping you, will truly understand the outcome you're hoping to achieve.

It's a lot easier to achieve a goal you can envision and articulate. You'll actually know when you're winning.

Therefore, we encourage you to answer this question and 3 others so you know exactly:

- **What do you want your marketing efforts to do for your organization?**

   What's the most pressing outcome you seek from your marketing efforts? For example, are you a local business or practice looking to attract more visitors from the community? Focus on selling more products and services to existing customers? Cultivate referrals? Develop a powerful loyalty program? Launch a successful new product line on the web?

   By identifying precisely what you're trying to accomplish and by when, you'll have an easier time developing tactics and messages that focus on those goals.

- **Who are your ideal target customers or prospects?**

   Businesses and veterinary practices marketing to pet owners:

   What types of people are you trying to attract to your location in person and online? Are they dog owners, cat owners, horse owners? Dog agility-competition fans? Hobby horse farmers? People who love green/organic pet products and services? People looking to adopt a pet? All of the above? Are they clueless about what you offer or do they already know what your business is all about?

What are they searching for when it comes to your products or services? What do you know about their lifestyles, interests, attitudes, hopes and needs — especially related to pets? What do they know about the "brand reputation" your business strives for?

The more you know about your target market, the more you can create powerful marketing materials that really hit home to their needs. In other words, you can position your store, facility or website to be a hero to those people! After all, they have other choices for pet-related solutions. (More on that in Chapter 2.)

Pet-industry and veterinary suppliers:

What type of companies and decision makers are you trying to sell your products or services to?

What are they searching for in regards to your solutions? What do you know about their lifestyles, interests, attitudes, hopes and needs — especially related to their business needs such as running a successful business or practice? What do they know about the "brand reputation" your company strives for?

The more you know about your target market, the more you can create powerful marketing materials that really hit home to their needs. In other words, you can position your business as the best supplier for them. After all, they have other choices for suppliers. (More on that in Chapter 2.)

* **What does your competition's marketing look like?**

Pet business and veterinary practices marketing to pet owners:

Have you studied competitors, such as other retailers, service providers or product developers who do a great job with their marketing? Or, those who do a terrible job?

Suppliers to the pet and/or veterinary industry:

Have you researched the other vendors marketing to your prospects? Since you and your competitors are going after the same market… how can you do it better or in a way that uniquely solves a problem? What can you offer that others don't?

The more you know about your competition for local, regional or even national choices, the more you can determine how to stand out from them and provide a superior solution to your target market. We'll show you how in this guide.

* **What have you tried before that works? Or, doesn't work?**

Right now, which of your marketing efforts — such as your website, Facebook page, email campaigns, print ads, direct marketing postcards or any other tools — work fairly well in driving visits and sales?

And, which of your efforts have been fairly disappointing when it comes to results?

If more of your efforts lean toward the disappointing side, don't worry. We're here to help you change that pattern.

Before your head starts spinning from all these questions, we're happy to tell you that we've developed great tools throughout this guide to help you figure all this out.

Now, it's time to begin building your itinerary.

Hang on — it's going to be a fun journey!

The worksheet on the next few pages is the beginning of your path to marketing success.

This worksheet asks you to identify the most critical aspects of your mission for growth: your purpose, goals, identity, uniqueness and the reasons why your current visitors and customers love you and why your prospects will, too... once they know about you.

This worksheet is not to be taken lightly.

It really is the foundation of your entire marketing roadmap. You'll want to take time to carefully consider each question and provide detailed information.

Ready? Let's begin building your Profit Producing Planner now.

 **WORKSHEET**

Define your Ultimate Destination
(Confirm Your Business Mission and Unique Value)

Part 1: Company Information

Organization name: _____

Marketing contact name: _____

Address: _____

City: _____ State: _____ Zip: _____

Phone: _____ Fax: _____ Cell: _____

Website Address (URL): _____

Email Address: _____

# of years in business: _____ # of employees: _____ # of customers: _____

Describe what makes your business special or different, in 4 sentences or less.
For example, what sights, sounds, feelings, outcomes and other experiences do you offer that your audience may not find anywhere else?

Where are you now:

What types of products, services and solutions do you offer?

[Example: all-natural dog food and treats, a website with luxury pet supplies, a membership/rewards program, training services, grooming services, pet cleaning supplies, innovative medical solutions, etc.]

How's business? Describe your current business climate. (What are the trends? What's popular?) [Example: Organic and natural pet food sales are expected to grow 3 times as fast as pet food sales overall through 2015 (Packaged Facts data).]

Describe your current market position in your geographic region if you depend on local business. (Where do you currently stand?) [Example: There are 3 major pet supply stores that compete for pet-parent dollars. People don't think to come to our boutique pet supply store more than once every few weeks or months.]

What barriers do you have to overcome — what might stop pet parents from visiting your retail store, doggie daycare, grooming facility or website… or what might stop pet companies or veterinary practices from buying your solutions? [Example: There are many competitors in our territory or market category, or potential visitors can't find our website in the search engines, etc.]

What makes your products or services unique or special in the buying landscape? What's the biggest benefit or unique solution you offer customers or target prospects? [Example: Of all the leash and collar companies selling products online, ours is the only one offering hand-tooled leather products that can be personalized with the pet's name and other finishing touches such as chrome accents.]

What were your organization's top 3 accomplishments during the last year regarding business growth?

What were the top 3 growth challenges your organization faced last year?

What did your organization fail to achieve last year with its marketing?

Clarify your business vision — what drives your current sales and your future:

* What types of programs, experiences, products and/or services do you really want to provide and promote?

* What is your organization's history?

* Where do you want your revenue and position to be at the end of the year? (In other words, what's your biggest marketing wish for the coming year?)

* What are your primary marketing goals? Let's get super-specific by setting 3 to 6 [S.M.A.R.T.] marketing objectives to grow your company. They need to be:
  * Specific
  * Measurable
  * Actionable
  * Realistic
  * Time-based

  Example: Increase monthly sales 12% within the next 12 months, or sell 125 widgets this month.

Now set your yearly marketing objectives:

1.

2.

3.

4.

5.

CHAPTER 1 SUMMARY/ACTION ITEMS
Define Your Ultimate Destination

❦ A successful marketing journey begins with a clear picture of your business goals.

❦ Start by asking yourself these critical questions:

- What do you want your marketing efforts to DO for your organization? (This is the most important question.)

- Who are your ideal target prospects, and what are they searching for in regards to your organization?

- What does your competition's marketing look like?

- What have you tried before that works? Doesn't work?

- What are your business/growth goals for the next year?

❦ By mapping out your current business situation and your marketing goals, you're well on your way to developing your Profit Producing Planner, one that actually works!

CHAPTER 1 Additional Notes:

chapter  **2**

Track Your Competitors

Understand the other dogs in the pack so you can race ahead of them.

Here's an important question for you: Do you know what your competition is doing?

For every pet business or veterinary practice, there's a group of online and offline competitors working hard to capture your customers' and prospects' attention and steer them away from you. They might be in the same town or across the world, depending on your business.

It's absolutely critical to study your competitors.

It's the only way to know how to position your location, organization and website in the crowded marketplace, make your products or services MORE attractive regarding price or special benefits, and create strong marketing messages that clearly set you apart for prospects and customers.

To study your competitors online, follow these easy steps to get started:

1. **Search in Google, Bing or another search engine using phrases relevant to your business.** Examples: If you're a dog agility center, check out "dog agility centers in [your state]." If you're a dog

grooming business, type in "[your city] dog groomer." If you make veterinary scrubs, type in "veterinary scrubs."

2. **Examine the first page results; who's listed there?** This includes all results, even the "sponsored ads" at the very top and in the right column. These competitors are paying to be found on page 1, as we'll explain shortly.

3. **Click on each listing and check out the website it leads to... using the questions we provide below.**

   - What products and services do they offer?

   - How can you do it better or in a way that uniquely attracts more people?

   - What can you offer that others don't?

The following worksheet will help you gather specifics about your top competitors. For starters, use a separate worksheet for each competitor. We recommend you identify 3 online and 3 in-person competitors (if you depend on local business).

WORKSHEET

Competitor Evaluation Sheet

Competitor (Other pet businesses or veterinary practices in your community and/or online):

Business name: _____

Marketing contact name: _____

Address: _____

City: _____ State: _____ Zip: _____

Phone: _____ Fax: _____ Cell: _____

Website Address (URL): _____

Email Address: _____

# of years in business: ____ # of employees: ____ # of customers: _____

Brief description of their business:

List their primary products/services | and prices

_____ | _____

_____ | _____

_____ | _____

_____ | _____

_____ | _____

What do they offer that's similar to your business?

What do they offer that's unique or different from your business?

What are their strengths?	What are their weaknesses?
_____	_____
_____	_____
_____	_____
_____	_____
_____	_____

On a scale of 1-10, how user-friendly is their website?

WORKSHEET

Fill in the following table to compare your business to your local and online competitors.

	YOUR COMPANY	COMPETITOR #1	COMPETITOR #2	COMPETITOR #3
PRODUCTS OR SERVICES				
PRICES				
TARGET CUSTOMERS				
MARKET POSITION				
MARKETING TACTICS				
TAGLINE OR SLOGAN				

Summarize the results of your competitor research:

Which competitor is the market leader?

Which is the weakest?

What's your unique position or offering that differentiates you from competitors?

List any media being used by the competition: radio, TV, print advertising, website, direct mail, etc.

Which social media venues are they using (Facebook, Twitter, YouTube, etc.)?

How does your competition promote itself through a tagline or slogan, such as "Your only natural cat food resource in (local area)" or "Easy-to-use veterinary practice management software"?

What do their marketing materials look like?

How can you communicate your offerings more effectively; in a way that uniquely solves a desire or problem for your prospects and customers? We'll talk more about this in Chapter 4.

Next, let's find out who needs to know about you.

CHAPTER 2 SUMMARY/ACTION ITEMS
Track Your Competitors

❧ It's critical to know what your competition is doing so you can set your business apart.

❧ There are four critical questions to ask yourself (use our worksheets in the Appendix to organize your answers):

- Who are your top 3 local competitors (if applicable) and top 3 online competitors?

- What's their market position and how do you compare?

- What does their marketing look like?

- What do you offer that's unique or better?

❧ By studying your competition, you can define your unique business position that stands out as the best choice.

CHAPTER 2 Additional Notes:

Know Your Target Audience

**Clearly define who you want to attract —
and why they'll choose you over other options.**

There's a famous saying in marketing, "You can't be all things to all people." You wouldn't even want to try! Your organization is designed to meet a specific market need, right?

So now you need to ask yourself, WHO is my marketing directed toward?

For better marketing results, you need to know exactly who your target prospects are, what they desire, and where you can find them.

In other words, you need to know their stripes.

In the marketing landscape, your target prospects are considered "searchers." This is because they may be out there right now, searching for the very thing your organization provides. They just don't know how to find you!

Here are some examples of possible searchers for pet products and services:

* A family looking to adopt a rescue dog or cat.

- A busy mom searching for quality doggie daycare within a reasonable budget.

- A Baby Boomer and Empty-Nester looking to connect with horses; something she always loved and now has the time to do.

- First-time pet parents looking for tips on how to raise a healthy puppy.

- A young rider training for 3-day equine eventing competitions.

Here are some examples of possible searchers for suppliers in the pet or veterinary industry:

- A pet professional starting a local pet bakery, looking for retail fixtures, signage, a point-of-sale system and other store needs.

- A pet-product entrepreneur looking for distributors to carry his unique inventions.

- A condo property manager searching for eco-friendly, sustainable furnishings and fixtures for an off-leash dog park.

- A veterinary practice manager looking for a more efficient computer system to manage electronic medical records, reminders and billing.

Get the idea? We're all searchers in the marketing jungle.

So, consider this: **Right now, your ideal target prospects are searching for a solution to their particular needs... and you can help them.**

That's why it's important to know exactly who your target prospects are, segment them into groups and supply their needs.

The better you understand this, the more you can speak to those searchers through marketing materials that are carefully chosen for the media that will reach them.

And the better you can attract them to your business or organization so they can enjoy all you have to offer.

In Chapter 1, we asked you to describe your typical current visitor or customer. Is this the kind of person who will also be your ideal target prospect? Or, will it be different as you look to increase your range of customers?

The following worksheet is designed to help you answer those questions and more.

WORKSHEET

Know Your Target Audience
(Define the Searchers You're Trying to Attract)

Here are the key questions that help you better understand your ideal prospects:

- **What types of people or businesses are you trying to attract to your organization's various offerings?** [List everything you can about them: gender, age, geographic location, etc.]

- **What are their characteristics?** [List their lifestyles, buying habits, hobbies, etc.]

- **Are they sophisticated, knowledgeable consumers regarding your offerings... or do you need to educate them?** [For example, do they already use all the items or services you offer or are you breaking new ground with them?]

- **What do you know about their interests, attitudes, hopes and needs — especially related to your various offerings?** [For example, are they excited about your products or services... or had they not even considered them?]

- **What major "pain" or need do they have that your organization can alleviate or address (what keeps them up at night)?** This will be different for each target: pet parents, pet-supply store owners, veterinary practices, etc. [For example, someone with an aging dog is hoping to ease their pet's aching joints and maintain a good quality of life in the golden years.]

- **What solution are they looking for?** [For example, are they looking for something that's easier, cheaper, faster; or something that will make them be a hero by keeping their pets healthy and happy? To be specific as possible, go back to pages 48–49 to review the examples of what searchers are looking for.]

- **How do your products or services offer the BEST solution for these prospects?** [For example, is it the easiest, cheapest, fastest, most reliable, most attractive or meaningful solution? This is where it really pays to know your competition and what they offer.]

Use "Personas" to picture your prospects

Here's one of the most helpful tips we've seen when it comes to knowing your target prospects.

Many companies create profiles or "Personas" of their target prospects. Think of them as mini "bios" that list each prospect's demographic profile, lifestyle and even attitude regarding your organization (or type of organization).

This background information can help everyone on your team "see" the target prospects you're trying to attract. It can also help writers, designers and marketers create materials designed just for those markets.

In fact, you may want to add a web page to your site that talks to each audience... for example, a first-time pet parent learning the basics of puppy care.

In short, Personas can help you save money and increase your marketing effectiveness because your messages will truly resonate with your audiences.

Here's a *Persona Profile* example for a company whose Ideal Customer is a female Baby Boomer traveler who loves dogs:

Persona Profile

Ideal Customer: Deborah Dog-Lover
Pet Lover, particularly dogs
Busy Boomer
Empty-Nester
Travel Enthusiast

- Female
- 50-60 years old
- 57% are married; 43% are single, divorced or living with a significant other

- Grown children
- Annual household income: $50K-$125K; still working full- or part-time
- Limited budget, yet she finds the resources to travel at least once a year
- Care for her pets is a priority (spends approximately $1,000-$2,000 a year on care, toys, accessories, doggie daycare and other pet-related expenses)
- Plus, she contributes to animal welfare organizations, from the local shelter to national ASPCA fundraising campaigns
- Reads pet and travel magazines: *Dog Fancy, The Bark, Traveler*
- Uses the Internet to find pet products, services, travel ideas and pet care answers
- Looking for pet-friendly hotels and services throughout the U.S.

Here's a *Persona Profile* example for a supplier prospect: a local doggie daycare owner who also offers boarding and grooming services.

Persona Profile

Ideal Customer: David Doggie Daycare Owner
Offers a high-quality facility and services to a local community
Busy business owner wearing many hats
Manages a staff of 9
Wants to grow his business through "add-on" services
Looking for a variety of services and products related to his business

- Male
- 32-52 years old
- Annual revenue: $290,000
- 8-12 years in the business
- Built the business from scratch
- Has a basic website, hopes to upgrade it this year

- Uses local advertising plus Facebook and his website
- Looking to expand by offering retail products and extra services
- Already has a groomer on staff
- Uses the Internet to find the right supplies and solutions to run his business
- Local competition is fierce
- Worries about maintaining growth

Persona Principles: Summarize your ideal customer or types of customers by...

- Age and sex
- Job or role
- Lifestyle
- Solution he/she seeks related to your organization
- Desire or hopes he/she has related to the solution
- Other choices he/she may consider

Start with your top 3 prospects.

We know that there may be many different types of audiences for you, including seasoned pet parents, first-time pet parents, pet professionals, veterinary practices, the media and others.

Therefore, we suggest that you focus on creating just 3 Personas to start with. Really dig in and have fun understanding what makes these 3 audiences tick.

Once you've created a set of Customer Personas for the 3 primary target audiences you wish to reach, share them with your team. Go through them together and also post them in work areas so the entire team gets to know these profiles. You can always add more later.

IMPORTANT POINTER

Make sure all your marketing efforts and messages speak to your prospects and customers as individuals on a personal basis, not as a group.

Think about it this way. Each person who reads your messages, views your website, or chats with you on Twitter is an individual.

Now you know who that individual is and what he or she seeks from you.

Stand out and surprise your prospects by talking to them in warm and personal ways. We'll show you how in the next chapter.

CHAPTER 3 SUMMARY/ACTION ITEMS:
Know Your Target Audience

- Identify their tracks: It's critical to know your ideal prospects and what they're searching for.

- Study their behaviors: The more you know about their concerns, wishes, hopes and desires, the easier it will be to create marketing materials that address those needs.

- Begin by asking these critical questions about your target audience(s):

  - What types of people are you trying to attract?
  - What are their characteristics?
  - Are they sophisticated, knowledgeable consumers who know what you offer... or do you need to educate them?
  - What do you know about their interests, attitudes, hopes and needs — especially related to your offerings?
  - What is their major "pain" or need your organization can alleviate or address?
  - What solution are they looking for?
  - How do your main products or services offer the BEST solutions for these prospects?

- Create a Persona for your top 3 ideal target prospects. Use those Personas to inspire marketing offers and messages that appeal directly to their personal wishes and desires.

CHAPTER 3 Additional Notes:

PART
II

Make sure your web foundation is solid,
since all marketing roads lead to it.

Quick. What are you focusing on right now in this photo?
We're guessing your full attention is on that heart-melting Maltese puppy, as it should be. You may not have noticed the background (the Jacksonville Airport waiting area) or the puppy-holder's wedding ring, or the intricate floor mosaic. Not at first. We feel fairly certain you were first captivated by the center of attention: that puppy face. Everything else is background. It's the same for your business. Your website is the center of your marketing efforts, since everyone will ultimately land there. That's what this section is about. (Airport puppy photo captured by Pam Foster)

This entire guide is about marketing, and it includes dozens of ideas on how to reach your audiences online and offline.

But, before you can do any effective marketing, consider this:

Everything leads to your website.

No matter how today's pet parents, pet businesses or veterinary practices find out about your organization, they'll head to your website to learn more, buy products, watch demo videos, inquire about your services and more.

This means your website is your #1 most important online marketing tool.

This was confirmed in the *PetAge* magazine 2011–2012 survey of pet retailers. 32 percent of survey respondents listed "Internet/website/email marketing/social media marketing" as their favorite form of advertising — up 10% from just a year before.

So, while you may have a great brand already, complete with logo, tagline and specific colors — the way your brand plays out online can be a whole different animal. A horse of a different color, so to speak.

This section is about your website — how it looks, feels and performs as the online representation of your brand — and how to make it a fantastic destination for your audiences.

Wow Them with Your Website

**Turn your site's visitors into happy customers
with a high-performing site you'll be wagging about.**

Your website's design and content will make — or break — your online success. Here's why.

At the very basic level, when potential customers arrive at your site, they want to know immediately what you offer, where you're located (if you rely on local business), how they can buy from you, and more.

If you're a supplier, your prospects and customers want to know what products you sell, how to get details, pricing and shipping info, and how can they order or learn more.

Consequently, there are three main web-success areas that must be addressed in your Profit Producing Planner. All are equally important for the "usability" (user-friendliness) and ultimate success of your site.

1. Site Architecture (Your site map)

This is the structure, functionality and fundamental usability of your website, including the navigation, number and type of pages, menu setup, any links or downloads, search capability, sign-up boxes, shopping cart process, forms and auto-responses, etc.

You need to create a site map to spell out all these things in detail — even if you currently have a website — because something might be out of whack. You'll be happy to know we've included a worksheet and some samples to help you do this. Read on!

2. Graphic Design (Your site's look and feel)

This is the look, feel and "readability" or reader-friendliness of your site, including colors, font choices, text formats, graphics and other design elements that reflect your organization's brand and help the viewer.

The graphic design blends your organization's identity (logo, etc.) with words, photos, charts and other visuals to help visitors move easily through your site to find what they need.

3. Web Content (Your site's messages)

Content refers to the actual words and messages that appear on each of your web pages to support your business goals. This is all the information you provide visitors to help them understand what you offer, why you're a great resource, and how to do business with you.

Content includes any of the following: sales/promotional copy, descriptive copy, articles, press releases, special promotions, staff bios, product, exhibit and service-specific features, testimonials, photo captions and more. It also includes keywords that support search engine rankings and traffic, which we explain in this chapter and Chapter 6.

 IMPORTANT POINTER

A website is not the same as printed marketing materials.

Keep in mind that designing and writing websites is different from designing and writing printed marketing materials, mainly because of the way people use websites. Many wonderful graphic designers and copywriters who excel in the print world have no experience creating websites.

You'll want to bring your brand to life online with web professionals who'll do a great job for you. Here's a quick overview of what we mean. You'll find detailed information on web professionals in Chapter 5:

* **A skilled web designer** understands the do's and don'ts of web graphics, and how to properly use color, space, typography and images to HELP, not hinder, the user experience — all supporting your goal of attracting customers and making money on your site. This designer will take your brand logo and colors, and apply them to a website design that works.

* **A skilled web copywriter** knows how to engage visitors immediately upon arrival with clear, appealing messages… and show them why your business is a wonderful place to find the pet products and services they seek.

   A skilled pet copywriter uses clear, persuasive messages that lead visitors to actions such as choosing and buying your products, or contacting you to schedule services.

   Suppliers also benefit from professional copywriters who write content that attracts site visitors, explains product or service benefits, and generates leads or purchases.

The skills of professional web designers and copywriters are critical to the effectiveness or usability of your site. Therefore, be very careful when choosing your web team. Be sure they have experience (and samples) of websites they've created, along with client references. We cover this in detail in Chapter 5.

IMPORTANT POINTER

Usability Rules.

Before we go into each of the three main areas of website architecture, design and content in detail, it's important to know about website usability and what it means to the success of your site.

Your website is as important as your carefully selected products, the quality of your services, your best sales people, your commitment to customer service and the impression people have when they visit your local facility if you have a bricks-and-mortar location.

For example, if you sell products in a retail shop, you probably spend a lot of time making sure it's attractive to customers so they instantly see what you provide. In your shop, customers can find products quickly, with clearly marked prices and several displays that help the shopper put your products together. Your friendly staff is standing by to help and to answer questions and is always available to assist with a quick, smooth checkout.

Finally, you thank the customer for shopping your store and you offer a savings coupon toward a return visit. It all makes for a very pleasant customer experience. This means they'll likely return to buy more if they're local or passing through again, and they'll tell all their friends.

This is essentially what website usability means. It's the delightful experience a customer has when they go on your site… so they'll continue to buy from you and tell others.

Website usability is so important that thousands, if not millions, of dollars are spent continually on studies. Entire books, industry guidelines and businesses are based on this subject.

The simple fact is, if your site's not user-friendly — if your visitors can't find what they're looking for — there's no point in having it.

Think for a moment about websites you like and use regularly.

These sites probably make it easy for you to find what you need. They're easy to read and don't make you search around or click-through several pages to order a product or get more information. There's no guessing or wasted time on these sites. Everything's organized for your needs.

When customers and prospects visit your site, they should have the same experience.

Great website design contains the following usability considerations:

* A simple, clean design that focuses on customer needs versus overblown designs, overly wordy text or overbearing visual gimmicks.

* Easy navigation or access to the main features, without being too busy or confusing.

* Detailed information (other pages or links) within just 1 or 2 clicks to prevent frustration for the visitor.

* Appropriate and helpful graphics balanced with descriptive text.

* A logical information hierarchy, with menus that guide customers to what they need.

The classic book *Homepage Usability,* the web industry's usability "bible," written by gurus Jakob Nielsen and Marie Tahir, originally included 113 usability guidelines. And, many more have been added over the years as the web has evolved.

But don't worry, we won't overwhelm you with all 113+ standards in this book! We've boiled them down to 43 standards — updated with today's online marketing best practices.

Our top 43 essential requirements encompass your site's functionality (site architecture), visual approach (graphic design) and sales messages/search engine optimization (content).

We're sure that 43 points still sound like a lot, but you can quickly run through the list and visual examples, and identify opportunities to improve your site.

Our 43-Point Checklist for Your Web Marketing Excellence

Site identity:

1. Show your organization's name and logo in the upper left-hand corner or at least in the top masthead area.

2. Include a tagline that summarizes the main benefit your business or organization offers in a customer-focused benefit statement (such as, "The Original High-Density Foam Pet Ramps and Steps" as shown on the next page).

3. Include a marketing hook (headline) that emphasizes your organization's unique value and solutions from the visitor's point of view.

Here's an example that follows these best practices:

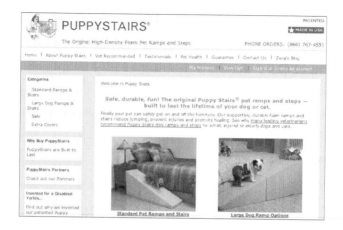

Company information:

4. Include an "About Us" page with location or company information.

5. Organize your information into standard/expected categories, such as:

   * Our Staff
   * Press Room
   * History

6. Present a unified face/brand to your audiences. All web pages and related marketing materials include your organization's brand look and "voice." (Everything needs to look like brothers and sisters.)

7. Include a "Contact Us" button that goes to a page with all contact information: email, phone and physical address, as well as live chat or other contact features.

8. Include a footer on every page with:

   * Organization name
   * Address
   * Phone
   * Live link to email

9. If your site gathers customer information, include a "Privacy Policy" page.

Here's an example that shows how some of these best practices are used. The arrows point out two ways to find the About Us page:

Content:

10. Use customer-focused language that explains the benefits of your business: what's in it for the visitor. Explain how you provide solutions or services in a way no one else offers. Or, if you're a supplier, show the special benefits of doing business with you.

11. Incorporate keywords into content in ethical, well-crafted messages, especially in the headline, subhead and other main areas. (See Chapter 6.)

12. Use "benefit-rich" bullets that make the content easy to scan.

13. Use uppercase letters sparingly for easier reading.

This clear, customer-focused content explains the benefits of an automated customer loyalty rewards program for pet retailers:

Links:

14. Differentiate links and make them stand out through bold and/or underline format (underlines are especially helpful for vision-impaired individuals). The only exception is your Social Sharing links. (See Point #42.)

15. Don't use generic instructions, such as "Click here," as a link name. Use specific beneficial action words instead, such as "Find your lost pet now."

16. Allow link colors to show visited and unvisited status, so your visitors remember whether or not they clicked on the link already. (Standard link colors: Blue #0000FF visitor has not been to yet, Purple #800080 visited link, Red #FF0000 active link)

17. If a link goes to a non-web page item such as a PDF, video clip, audio clip, email window, etc., add an icon or short caption indicating this so there are no surprises for the visitor.

The following example points to helpful links that stand apart from the other text online, with the keywords "natural dog food" and "natural cat food":

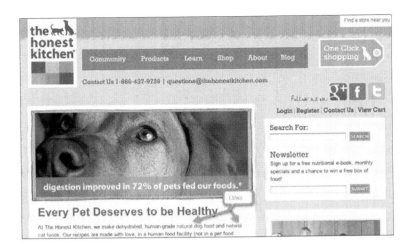

Navigation:

18. Make sure your primary navigation runs across the top of the page or down the left, never on the right. Reader studies prove that visitors expect your buttons to be placed in these locations for a user-friendly experience.

19. Group similar items together within navigation sections.

20. Use standard naming conventions: Home, About Us, Products, Services, Directions, Contact Us. Don't use made-up words for button names; it may confuse visitors.

21. If you sell products on your website, place the shopping cart buttons in the upper right-hand side of the main masthead so people see it on every page. The most popular button names are:

- Your account
- Shopping cart
- Check out

This website has a very clear and clean navigation, with a Shopping Cart indicator on the upper right, product categories grouped together logically, and other best practices:

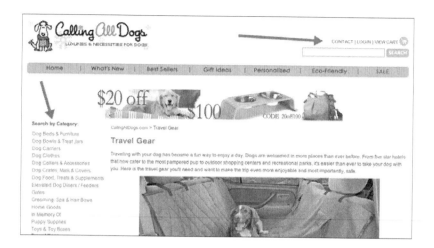

22. Add a site map, which helps visitors and search engines know what's on your website.

This site has a nice, clear site map:

Search boxes within your site: If you offer a search function on your site...

23. Give users a SEARCH box on the home page (so they can quickly find what they are looking for), not a link to a search page.

24. Use a "search" or "go" button to the right of the box.

25. Don't offer a "search the web" feature. In general, don't link people to other websites. Why would you want visitors to leave your site?

This website has an easy-to-find SEARCH feature on every page:

Graphics and animation:

26. Optimize graphics to web-appropriate sizes (72 dpi is recommended). Be aware that large files slow down page viewing and annoy visitors. (In fact, search engines punish slow-loading sites.)

27. Use photos that relate to the content, not just as decorations or irrelevant entertainment.

28. Let users choose whether they want to see an animated intro to your site! Don't make it the default.

29. Video and audio should be in the off position. Give users the option of turning them on with a clear PLAY button. Even better, offer a MUTE button for the sound.

This website does a nice job of balancing graphics and messaging:

Graphic design:

30. Limit font styles to 2 or 3 maximum per site. Over-designing the site can be distracting to the user.

31. Use black type on a white background for easy reading... especially for the body text where there's lots of copy.

32. Avoid forcing visitors to do horizontal (side-by-side) scrolling at 800 x 600 screen size.

33. The most critical page elements should be visible "above the fold" — on the first screen visitors see when they land on your web pages. (Above the fold is a graphic term that refers to placing graphics in the upper half of the web page.)

34. Make sure pages rarely force the visitor to scroll more than 2.2 times. (Exception: sales-letter landing pages.)

35. Avoid using pop-up windows. Yes, some companies swear by them. But most web visitors find them to be distracting and annoying. (A recent study identified them as one of the "top hated" online marketing techniques.)

Here's a website design that's very clear, user-friendly and does a nice job of balancing graphics and messaging:

Communicating unfinished pages:

36. If parts of your website are not finished, add a date of when they will be finished. (Statistics show that when a viewer goes to a page under construction you have a 12% chance of having that person come back to your site. Yuck.)

SEO (search engine optimization) basics (we cover SEO in detail in Chapter 6):

Make sure every page of your site includes these unique and relevant behind-the-scenes "meta tags":

37. Title tag with keywords/keyphrases. (70 characters/spaces maximum; real sentences are best)

38. Header tags with keywords/keyphrases. (Headline = H1 Tag, Subhead = H2 Tag)

39. Meta description using keywords/keyphrases in a complete sentence or two (this may be displayed in search engines; limit to 150 characters/spaces)

40. Keyword tag. (Ideally no more than 10 keyword phrases)

41. Alt tags with keywords/keyphrases. (for charts, photos and other graphics that aren't text)

This website is optimized with various versions of "pet insurance" keywords:

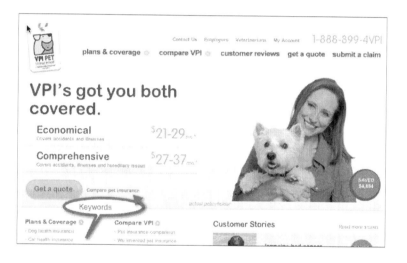

And here's how this page's Page Title and Meta Description appear in Google search results:

VPI **Pet Insurance** | Shop for Pet Health Care Insurance Plans ...
www.petinsurance.com/
VPI provides various **pet insurance** plans for dogs, cats and other exotic pets. 9 out of
10 veterinarians who recommend **pet insurance** recommend VPI. Learn ...
VPI Pet Insurance Forms. - Contact Us - Plans & coverage - Dog Insurance Plans

Social Media:

42. Place your social media buttons/links prominently at the top of each page (see the Red Bank Veterinary Hospital example below). Or, in the upper part of your right-hand margin. Also, invite people to join you and share any benefits they may receive as a follower.

43. Include an invitation to subscribe to your blog by email and/or RSS feed, and also to share posts in social media. The best placement is also in the upper right part of your right-hand column.

In this screen shot, you'll see that the social media buttons for Facebook, Twitter, YouTube, and the RSS Feed are prominently displayed just beneath the masthead so they can't be missed.

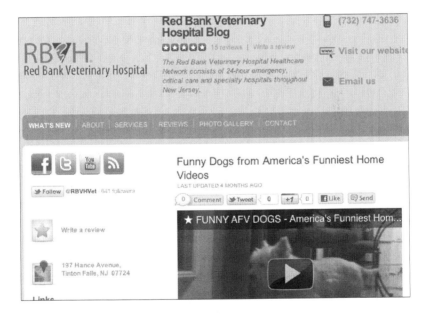

How does your site measure up against this checklist?

Find out by using the *43-Point Checklist for Web Marketing Excellence* found in the Appendix section of your book. This tool helps you evaluate your website, item by item.

If you're serious about improving the user-friendliness and sales conversions on your site — leading to more visits and profits — we encourage you to complete this "do it yourself audit" or hire a professional web content auditor to provide a consultation with recommended improvements.

Now, let's dive into the design and content areas in more detail, so you can make further progress on your goals.

Site Architecture Considerations

Have you ever visited a site where you can't find what you want? Or, it takes more than 3 clicks to get to the page you need? How about not being able to locate contact information or basic facts? Worst of all, have you ever decided to order a product on a site, but had to jump through all kinds of frustrating hoops to do so, and ultimately gave up?

One of the biggest pet peeves people have with websites is a multi-step online ordering process that ends up with an error message after spending 10 minutes filling in all the required screens. Sheesh.

These problems are all the result of poor site structure or architecture. And believe us, you don't want these problems to happen to your prospects and customers.

A great site architecture clearly outlines all the functions and features you need on your site to have the best chance of generating profits. These functions and features may include:

- Interactive forms (order products online, sign-up for services, submit a contact form, etc.)
- Database for searching
- Ecommerce/catalog
- Links and downloads
- Discussion forum
- Video clips
- Blog

A great site architecture also determines all the pages (and types of pages) you need on your site, such as:

Example for a local pet business or veterinary practice:

- Home (Newsletter sign-up box and social media sharing buttons)
- About Us
  - Why Choose Us
  - Staff
  - History
  - Directions
  - Employment
- Products
  - Product Category (as many as needed, such as Food, Beds, Dishes, Leashes, Toys)
- Individual Product Detail Page (as many as needed)
- Services
  - Service Category (as many as needed, such as Boarding, Daycare, Grooming)
- Individual Service Detail Page (as many as needed)
- Programs
  - Pet Training Classes
  - Free Screening Clinics
  - New Puppy/Kitten Classes
- Articles and/or Videos
  - How-To or What's New articles related to your products or services
  - For veterinary practices, this may include health tips, warnings
- Blog
- Pressroom
  - Media Kit
  - Press Releases
  - Photos and Videos
- Support Us (if you're a nonprofit rescue shelter or other organization)
  - Membership
  - Donate

- Adopt an Animal
- Volunteer Opportunities
- Store (if you sell products online)
  - Sales Promotions/Special Offers
  - Shopping Cart
    - Your Account
    - Shopping Cart
    - Check Out
- FAQs
- Contact Us
- Site Map
- Privacy/Terms

Example for suppliers to the pet industry or veterinary practices:

- Home (Newsletter sign-up box and social media sharing buttons)
- About Us
  - Why Choose Us
  - Staff
  - History
  - Employment
- Our Products or Services
  - Include PDF spec sheets for easy download
  - Specials
  - Downloadable Order Forms
  - Pricing
  - Comparisons
- Articles
- Blog
- Video Training or Product Demos (if applicable)
- FAQs
- Pressroom
  - Media Kit
  - Press Releases
  - Photos and Videos
- Shopping Cart (if you sell products online)

- • Your Account
- • Shopping Cart
- • Check Out
- ❧ Contact Us

Authentic testimonials should be sprinkled throughout the site for best readability and relevance, and should include first name, last name and town. Also include all reviews, not just the positive comments — people respect that. After all, why would someone view a web page they know only has good stuff written about you?

IMPORTANT POINTER

Know the DO's and DON'Ts of profitable websites.

Your website should always have:

- ❧ Full organization name, address, phone and email address on every page. This builds trust with your customers. They want to know who you are, where you are and how to contact you.
- ❧ All important information no more than 2 clicks away.
- ❧ A way for the visitor to always return to the home page.
- ❧ A mobile-friendly version as soon as possible! (Talk with your web team about creating a phone-friendly site layout that's designed specifically for the small screen. See Chapter 9 for Mobile Marketing details.)

Pet business and veterinary sites should try to avoid:

- ❧ Automatic sound (talking or music: this is extremely risky and will turn off many visitors)
- ❧ Animation that's automatic (can be too distracting from your important messages)
- ❧ Background images (can be too distracting and make your messages hard to read)
- ❧ Tiny, hard-to-read text
- ❧ Black backgrounds with hard-to-read text

If you and your viewers consider your site to be ineffective and you know it needs updating, we urge you to try and remodel it as soon as possible using these guidelines.

Why?

Your website is your face to the world.

While you may think no one's really looking at it, every day, a visitor — perhaps even an ideal prospect for your products and services — could be checking it out and saying, "This place is not right for me."

A skilled web team will take your information and create a detailed architecture or site map that includes all the elements in a structure that supports optimum usability.

The following basic site map and wireframe show you what we mean:

Your Site Map
(The better prepared you are, the higher your chances for success.)

A site map — also known as a wireframe or schematic — clearly displays every page of your site along with the links and forms you'll include. Best of all, it shows how the pages will guide the user through the site and in what sequence.

We've included a very basic site map and wireframe example here. Your web team will create a customized site map for you after you meet with them.

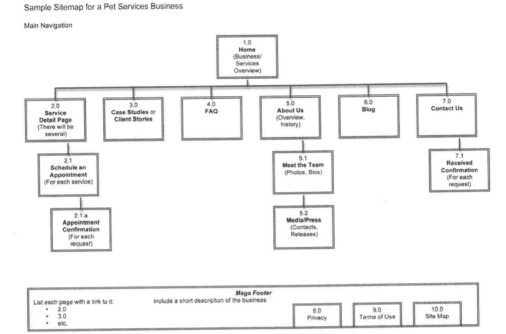

Sample Sitemap for a Pet Services Business

In the Appendix, you'll find a blank Site Map and Wireframe you can use to jot down your thoughts.

Graphic Design Considerations

Now let's look at your site's design from another perspective.

Have you ever gone to a site that had a 30-second Flash video greeting that asked you to "please wait while intro loads?"

Have you arrived at a home page to find a mish-mash of confusing text blocks, with no clear direction on where to look for what you need? Or, how about that all-black background with purple copy that's nearly impossible to read?

Our least favorite are those flashing messages with animated monkeys jumping all around — an instant headache! Even if the monkeys are cute.

These problems are the result of poor graphic design. The second half of your site design puzzle is how your site "looks and feels" from the customer's perspective.

To ensure that your website ROCKS and turns visitors into customers, we encourage you to work with a professional web designer who has a track record in creating websites that are easy to read and easy to use, with graphics that guide visitors through the decision-making sequence in a clear and quick way.

Here are some graphic design considerations that are unique to the web. It's a good idea for you to know these requirements so you're well prepared to work with your web designer.

IMPORTANT POINTER

Details your web graphic designer needs you to know:

- **About Colors:** There are 256 web-safe colors available that read properly on any computer monitor. Your designer will make every attempt to match your logo colors with the web-safe choices, but probably can't use your Pantone® colors or match them exactly. Check out www.webmonkey.com to view web-safe colors.

- **About Images:** Images must be provided or created in specific formats for proper display on the web. The three most common image file formats are .jpg, .gif and .png. (.bmp files offer excellent image resolution or sharpness, but they're too large for the web.)

  - .jpg files are the best for photos.
  - .gif is the most common type of file for graphic images.
  - .png offers excellent editing capabilities.

- **About File Sizes:** "File size" refers to how much space a file takes up on the server. For your web pages to load quickly (in 30 seconds or less) and provide customers with instant viewing, small file sizes — 80 KB or less for the entire page — are best. This topic may come up in your design discussion if you want to feature lots of photos or one huge image file on any given page of your site.

Colors, text fonts, numbers of clicks and many other aspects of your page are critical to your site's profitability, because they can either keep your visitors engaged or turn them away.

For the best results, be sure to include a skilled web graphic designer in your site assessment and adjustments or redesign.

Web Content Considerations

If you're expecting your website to prompt inquiries or drive orders for your products and services, you'll want to carefully plan your web content. Smart, sales-oriented and "optimized" content will ensure the best results for your site.

Content is King (or Queen)

"Content is King" has become the rule of thumb on the Internet because the content, or copy, is your online salesperson.

When web copy engages prospects immediately and clearly shows them all the appealing services and/or products you offer, the results can be very exciting.

Profitable web content includes copy that meets your visitors' expectations at all levels of contact — from your site's description in Google searches to the promises you make on each web page.

Without great copy, many prospects become confused or frustrated and leave your site.

7 Fundamental Guidelines to Creating Great Web Content

Here are 7 fundamental guidelines to creating great web content, and ultimately, ensuring the online sales results you desire.

1. **Write for your customers and tell them how you'll meet their needs.**

Customers will not be excited about a pet business, veterinary practice or pet-industry organization that talks all about itself: "We do this, we do that." This is known as business "we-we."

The number one rule of successful website content is that it must focus on customers and offer clear solutions that meet their needs.

In other words, you must deliver a promise — a value proposition — right away or you'll lose your visitors within seconds.

For example, let's say you sell a series of programs specifically designed to help new dog owners learn how to train their pups for the first time. Your first instinct might be to say on your home page:

> **We offer courses on training your dogs to behave.**
> **We've been doing this for years.**
> **We're really great at it.**

The customer will see this and say, "But, what kind of courses? What will I learn from them? How easy or hard are they? How will the courses help me?"

Instead, if your content is written for the customer, you might say the following:

> **New to dog ownership?**
> **Teach your dog basic obedience skills in just 3 evenings.**

With our easy, helpful tools and guidance, you'll know how to get your dog to sit, stay, come when you call and not jump on people.

See the difference? This content clearly identifies the audience (new dog owners) and offers a unique, specific promise that solves their need.

This is the concept behind the USP, the Unique Selling Proposition, which we also like to call your Unique Solution Proposition.

IMPORTANT POINTER

Know your USP.

Your Unique Selling Proposition, or Unique Solution Proposition, can help you differentiate your business to attract more customers and profits.

In the 1940s, Rosser Reeves of the ad agency Ted Bates & Company, coined the USP to help clients develop unique selling points and build brand appeal, recall and hopefully, sales. (Source: Wikipedia)

Mr. Reeves' definition of the Unique Selling Proposition was,

1. "Each advertisement must make a proposition to the customer: 'Buy this product, and you will get this specific benefit.'

2. The proposition itself must be unique — something that competitors do not, or will not, offer.

3. The proposition must be strong enough to pull new customers to the product."

Paige Arnof-Fenn, an accomplished international marketing and branding expert and founder of Mavens & Moguls, recently spoke at a business meeting we attended in Boston. She said, "People aren't surfing the Net anymore, they're searching for very specific solutions."

That's exactly it! It's about solutions.

So, we're going to make the radical suggestion that we call the USP your **Unique Solution Proposition.**

Ultimately, when all is said and done, people who are the ideal prospects for your organization are looking for a terrific solution — whether it's a great local resource for pet care, the perfect gift for an pet-lover, or a specific service that makes their job easier.

In fact, it's really even deeper than that.

You'll be a hero by providing a solution that helps people celebrate pets and keep them healthy and happy.

So, how do you craft your USP? Here's a formula that may help.

My [define your organization]_____ is the
only one that [offers what solution]_____
for [define your audience] _____
by [how: explain your unique product or service] _____

_____ .

Here's an example of what this may look like for a local pet supply business that's committed to supporting safe, all-natural products, services and practices.

"Our pet supply business is the only local eco-friendly resource providing pet essentials (food, treats, dishes, bedding, toys and gifts) in a totally green environment, to people who care about natural resources and sustainability."

A tagline or slogan (aka, a promise statement) that might be developed from this USP statement might be:

Pet-friendly. Earth-friendly.

A headline that might be developed from this USP statement might be:

Celebrate your pet's health and happiness with our safe, all-natural pet foods and supplies!

It's pretty clear how this store sets itself apart from other local pet businesses, right? That's the power of a USP.

If you don't have a USP for your organization (most businesses don't!), or you have one that could use some updating, try using our formula.

Also, be sure the copy is written in a voice that reflects your organization's brand. Again, your brand is the image or perception you build in your prospects' and customers' minds — it's the combination of the identity graphics (logos, colors), messages, tangible products and intangible experiences your business presents to your audiences again and again.

Your voice or tone should be consistent throughout your site and all your marketing materials. It can be one of many styles, including friendly, sophisticated, down-to-earth, upbeat, authoritative, excited, serious or nurturing, funny, quirky, etc.

2. **Make sure your content is written for people who have little time and even less patience.**

Keep in mind that people come to your site to find solutions as quickly as possible.

Statistics show that web visitors scan sites for **just 3 to 6 seconds** — and then decide whether they'll read on or move on. So, if they can't rapidly find the information they need, they'll move on.

This means, in most cases, NO big splashy Flash graphics on your home page!! The web industry has proved it again and again: Flash intros can take too long to load and can be very distracting. (Apple doesn't even support Flash graphics in its iPad technology.) Many prospects will move to another site when there's a delay or an annoying visual in their way.

Also, a fancy "intro" page that's heavy on graphics and limited on copy can be very frustrating for a busy web visitor because, again, it can take an "eternity" to load. Make sure design gimmicks aren't driving your prospects away.

The best pet business-related websites have a strong headline, followed by short sentences, subheads and bullets to break up copy and make it easier to read. Product descriptions are very brief and skillfully written to build interest. Charts, tables and other graphics help support the copy in a user-friendly, quick-scan way.

3. **Provide a customer-benefit headline and/or subhead at the top of every page on your site.**

Again, your prospects are looking to find out what you can do for them. Make sure your very first message demonstrates that you understand their wishes and can please them better than anyone else. Or, that you offer them a clear benefit or promise they'll be interested in.

Below, you'll see an example of a web page that immediately explains the product lines many benefits to the target prospect. Even the business name includes benefits: Safe and Dry.

"Welcome" is not a headline!

"Welcome to our site" does not give your prospects any information about what you can do to help them. "Choose from the world's largest selection of dog breed-specific gifts" is a much more beneficial promise for the prospect.

Another good example is: "Earn exclusive discounts today with our referral program." That's a direct benefit that's targeted to your customer. What pet parent doesn't want to earn exclusive discounts on products they regularly buy?

So, let's say this out loud together, right now: "Goodbye, Welcome headline! Hello, profit-generating headline!"

4. Remember that people buy exciting benefits and value, not features.

The ultimate goal of your prospects and customers might be to treat their beloved pets, run a successful veterinary practice, find help for a pet problem, etc. It's these ultimate benefits that you need to focus on when promoting your organization's products and services.

For example, using an autopilot customer loyalty rewards program isn't just a convenience for a pet-supplies retailer — it saves precious time and ultimately helps reduce stress while bringing in more sales.

Make sure you're thinking about the benefits of your programs, products and services this way.

This is the key to what's known today as "conversion optimization." This means that more prospects "convert" to paying customers: product buyers, qualified sales-leads, members or other active participants in your business.

If people land on your site and DON'T convert to buying customers, your site's content isn't pleasing them. It isn't "conversion optimized." So, your web content needs to be people-friendly as well as search-engine friendly.

Here's a wonderful example of inviting web copy that's written to convey benefits and paint a picture for prospects:

Meadowbrook Kennel & Spa, Damariscotta, Maine

This lovely "home away from home" dog boarding facility is located on a property that offers opportunities for 2-3 walks daily, exploring the trails winding thru meadows, woods, wetlands and visiting Pemaquid Lake.

Each delightfully appointed suite (12'x12') includes a sofa and dog bed for your dog's relaxing pleasure while listening to classical music. The adjacent half-acre play area affords supervised outdoor time to have activities of their choosing: ball fetching, walking, rolling in the grass or just sleeping in the sun. Massages and swimming are available upon the owner's request. Oooh. Sounds like a wonderful place for dogs and people! But only dogs are allowed. You'll have to find your own spa.

Owner Ginny Libby tells us, "Meadowbrook Kennel & Spa is so valued that some people book up to a year ahead for the holidays or a special trip to ensure that their dog gets to get a suite here. Call (207)563-1475 to make an appointment for your pup, to stop by for a tour. You can also join their Facebook page to see what's new and see fun photos of the dogs relaxing there.

Make sure your strongest and most unique benefits are "above the fold" on your web page. This is the area visitors see on their screen first when they land on your site. Keep in mind that the "fold line" may be different depending on each visitor's monitor size, browser window, selected screen size and more. But in general, it's the top section of any page, before scrolling is required.

Here's an example of what we mean by the area "above the fold."

5. Include credibility so prospects will feel comfortable buying from you.

After you've made your promise and explained how you offer the best solution for your prospects' needs, add sources of credibility to back it up, such as:

* Photographs of your friendly staff, pets using your products or services, etc.

* Information about your company's history, special services, dedication to pet care.

* Your story — the story of your company. Tell visitors why you chose to be in your business and what you offer that's special. People love stories, especially about others who love pets!

* Media coverage you've received, with logos of the media firms (newspapers, websites, TV shows, etc.).

* Comparison page: consider listing all the amenities or benefits of your business compared to those of your competitors… making sure you outshine the competition, of course!

* A long list of satisfied customers, with testimonials and photos of them enjoying your solutions.

Customer testimonials are a form of "social proof" that can be very powerful toward building credibility. When your prospects see how other people have enjoyed your specific products or services, they'll be able to envision themselves enjoying the same benefits.

Testimonials must be real and believable. Keep them short, include specific benefits or results your business provided them, and include full names, locations, and even photographs whenever possible.

Here's a terrific example of a website section that includes several credibility elements:

6. Invite prospects and customers to sign up for your enewsletter.

Are you familiar with the 80/20 rule? On the web, many businesses are finding that most of their sales (80%) come from repeat customers (the 20% of their loyal buyers). And yet, MANY businesses don't have a mechanism for following up with their best customers.

One easy way to fix that problem is to build customer relationships by collecting email addresses and then regularly sending out fresh news or members-only offers.

In a recent study, 69% of web users reported that they look forward to receiving at least one email newsletter, and most users said a newsletter had become part of their routine. (Source: Nielsen Norman Group Report on Email Newsletter Usability)

The report stated, "Newsletters feel personal because they arrive in users' in-boxes, and users have an ongoing relationship with them. Very few other promotional efforts can claim this degree of customer buy-in." We'll dig into emails and enewsletters in Chapter 8.

For now, to collect email addresses, all you need to do is put an inviting enewsletter sign-up box on your home page as well as on your Order Confirmation page (or ideally on every page if possible). To motivate signups, include an attractive offer that people will receive if they opt-in, such as a free pet-care guide or report that has appeal and value to your prospects.

Here's a very simple, compelling example of what a newsletter sign-up form looks like. Who doesn't want to be a savvy shopper?

7. Make it very easy for customers to buy from you and contact you.

This one can be the simplest to do. If you sell products online, make sure your site includes ample invitations to "order now." Then, make the ordering process as simple as possible, with as few clicks and fill-ins as possible. A 5-step ordering process just isn't the best for your customers. Make it a 2- or 3-step process at the most.

Finally, if you're trying to generate sales leads on your site, give customers an irresistible reason and easy method for signing up. Use a simple sign-up box on the home page, so people won't have to click several times.

Be sure to collect only the information you need for successful follow-up. It's proven that the "form abandon rate" increases with each additional data field people are required to fill in. All you really need to collect is First Name, Last Name, and Email Address... plus maybe one more field asking for a "Reason for Your Inquiry" if applicable.

Remember that Content is King and can work wonders to drive more visits and revenue.

Professional content is well worth the investment. If you're not a skilled web copywriter and you don't have a copywriter on your staff, you'll want to add a professional web content consultant and Certified SEO copywriter as a vital part of your web development team. (See Chapter 5.)

Now, it's time to collect the specific background information needed for site improvements or new pages that excel.

Introducing The Web Creative Brief

In just a moment, you'll have access to one of the world's best web marketing tools: the *Web Creative Brief*.

This carefully crafted document and marketing foundation helps you outline all the important design and message considerations needed to make your site successful. It gives you and your web team a clear, focused roadmap for developing your site's personality.

A good Web Creative Brief will contain your organization's brand information, its Unique Selling Proposition or Unique Solution Proposition (USP) to the customer, and a discussion of the current market situation and competition.

Why use a **Web Creative Brief?**

It's quite simple. **The Brief will dramatically increase your site's chances for success** because all parties — your own internal team and your professional web development team — can use it to clearly craft a solid site improvement plan that includes all your important elements for success.

There's no guessing. You'll all know exactly what to expect as you work through the details of each page.

Without a Web Creative Brief to guide every member of your marketing team and web development team, you'll likely wind up with:

- An end product that's very different from what you expected and needed

- A site that brings in poor response

- Heavy (and costly) revisions

- A disconnect from your various online and offline marketing efforts — weakening potential sales overall

- Wasted time and effort for everyone

- Barking up the wrong tree! (Not reaching your ideal prospects)

Take time now to review the Brief on the following pages, and even fill it in. This effort will reward you with clear thinking about the best way to promote your pet-related business. You'll also find the Web Creative Brief in the Appendix section.

WORKSHEET

The Web Creative Brief

(Identify the critical design elements and key messages for your site.)

PART 1: Current Situation

- Business marketing goals:

- Competitive climate:

- Barriers to overcome — what might stop customers from buying? (price, not aware, selection)

- What marketing efforts have worked? Not worked?

PART 2: Graphic Design Considerations

- What does your current brand look like? Describe in detail (or attach your Branding Guidelines):

- Logo:

- Color palette:

- Typography (fonts and styles):

- Imagery (illustration, art):

- Photography:

- Other considerations (use of white space, position of elements):

- What is the visual tone to be conveyed on your site? (light-hearted, fun, practical, bright, cheery, serious, authoritative, feminine)

- Does your audience already know your brand?

- What do your competitors look like on their sites?

- Do you own digital photographs for your products, services and people? If so, in what size and format?

- Do you own artwork/illustrations?

PART 3: Content/Message Considerations:

- What's the main UNIQUE benefit or solution only your facility, products and services can offer? (This is the USP, or Unique Selling Proposition/Unique Solution Proposition.)

- List the key features of your organization: what you offer.

- List the key benefits of your organization: the desired results or value of what you offer.

- How interested is the target audience in your events, products and solutions?

- What key "pains" of your target audience (problems or wishes), can you solve?

- What are you really selling? (e.g., you're not selling pet portraits/photography; you're selling a special image/heirloom that honors a beloved pet. Or, you're not selling innovative diagnostic blood analyzers to veterinarians; you're selling better medical answers so the practitioner can be a hero to his clients.)

- Are there any other emotional motivators you should consider (frustration, pride, greed)?

- What support or "reasons to believe" do you have for your key promise messages (testimonials, endorsements, case studies, product specifics, etc.)?

- What obstacles or objections do you need to overcome for success?

- What are your competitors offering?

- How can you set your business or organization apart from the competition? Why choose you?

- What's the proper, branded tone of "voice" for your messages? (serious, light-hearted, fun, practical)

- Does your audience know you? Will you need to address issues of credibility?

- What phrases (keywords) does your audience use to find your products or services in search engines… or what would you expect them to use?

- What is your call-to-action? Why should the audience respond NOW?

- How can the audience respond to you (phone/mail/web/mail/fax)?

Be sure to complete the Web Creative Brief in your Appendix to help guide your entire marketing team to success.

Now for the final consideration of updating and marketing your website: your budget.

Plan for the costs

Establish a reasonable budget for a customized, profit-generating site.

Let's have a drum roll, please...

Now it's time for us to reveal the first-ever, realistic discussion on what you can expect to pay for a professional website that's optimized and fully customized for your organization's needs...

and what you can expect to pay for monthly maintenance and marketing once your site is launched.

The web development community seems to shy away from revealing prices unless they're dirt-cheap. We're not sure why. But, we're here to tell you the truth up front with no surprises or hidden agendas.

The Template Approach

There's a selection of "one size fits all" template websites that certainly serve a purpose for small businesses with tiny budgets.

The trick with these templates is to make them your own by customizing the content and design so it's all about your specific services, local community (if applicable) and other unique aspects of your business.

WordPress is a popular platform. It's a free blog system that can be used for creating websites. Once you set up your basic format, you can add custom designs, images and content to make it uniquely yours.

One word of caution: When you consider using a template system, know your limitations for what you can do yourself. Unless you're a clever web programmer or you want to learn how to manage WordPress plugins, widgets and more — customizing can be tricky. It's best to hire a web expert to set up your site and then train you on how to add updates and make changes. This doesn't have to be expensive, and it's well worth the peace of mind that your site is functioning properly.

PetCopywriter.com is a WordPress site that Pam can go into at any time to add new pages, blog posts, PDFs and other updates. However, Pam is not a programmer, so she relies on her WordPress expert to regularly make sure the site is running properly for search engines and visitors.

While WordPress is the most popular do-it-yourself template platform, others worth checking out are www.BigCommerce.com (especially good if you have an online store), www.Weebly.com, www.Hostgator.com and www.Web123.com.

If you're responsible for a veterinary practice website — there are several companies/systems available just for you. For example, LifeLearn's WebDVM4 is a complete, turnkey system designed specifically for veterinary hospitals and clinics.

For a simple $699 set-up or license fee, plus a $125/month subscription, WebDVM4 gives your practice a web presence with everything your clients and prospects need to know about you.

Of course, it's up to you to customize the information specific to your practice and local area… but the WebDVM4 shell comes with a fresh, updated and SEO-friendly design that includes several styles you can easily customize. Plus, it includes functions such as social sharing, a blog, and ClientEd Online, which is a library of over 1,200 healthcare articles written by veterinarians to educate your clients. You can add other features if you wish for an additional setup and monthly fee. Lucky you! To learn more about this resource, visit: http://www.lifelearn.com/veterinary-practice-success/

The Big Bucks Approach

On the other end of the spectrum, there are companies that charge enormous elephant-size fees because they have in-house teams that develop fully customized sites complete with extensive bells and whistles. These are the "boutique" web firms that position themselves as the Tiffany's of web design companies.

We know that many of these firms may be well worth the cost to a huge pet-industry corporation or ecommerce business that needs a robust, fully-custom site, but most organizations find that it's not necessary to pay over $100,000 for a website.

We're pleased to tell you that a great, profitable site doesn't have to cost a fortune.

The Business-Friendly Approach

A great optimized site for many pet businesses and industry suppliers should cost between $15,000 and $30,000 on the lower end, and $30,000 to $80,000 or higher for a fully functional site including ecommerce, feedback, search capability, online applications, forums and other complex functions.

These prices are for the website development and launch. Ongoing maintenance and marketing are budgeted separately.

To put this into perspective, Internet Retailer recently surveyed a group of retailers, asking them how much they plan to spend on a website redesign, and how long they figured it would take. The survey included chain retailers, catalog companies, web/ecommerce sites, and product manufacturers. Here are the survey findings:

* **Why they're redesigning their sites:** 46.4% of the retailers are redesigning their websites to attract new visitors and shoppers; 53.1% are looking to boost sales, and 35.1% plan to generate higher sales conversions. (The retailers were asked to check "all that apply.")

- **What they expect to spend:** 67% of retailers expect to spend less than $50,000 on their redesign, while 22% expect to spend between $50,000 and $250,000.

- How much time it will take: 42.1% of retailers expect their update to take less than 3 months, while 37.6% are planning 3 to 6 months, and another 13.2% are spending 6 to 9 months.

Remember, an investment in a custom-built, high quality, fully optimized and marketing-focused site will more than pay for itself in the long run. We'll explain why in a few moments. First:

What you can get for $15,000-$30,000

You can expect to launch a professional, branded brochure site or customized lead-generation site that includes several pages about the benefits of your services or products, your team's background and expertise, the credentials of your firm (including photos and bios), examples of your programs, amenities and services; a contact page, helpful resources or PDFs, an enewsletter invitation page (if you choose to include one), customized content throughout, and of course, initial keyword research and placement.

What you can get for $30,000-$80,000 or more

Sites that include ecommerce and/or databases become more costly to create because they require more technology. If you offer several product lines, you'll need separate pages for each one. If you're adding extensive links, PDFs*, forms or other documents, discussion forums, calculators and more, that can add up too.

*PDF is short for Portable Document Format, which makes it possible to read formatted documents in a file that can be viewed by anyone who has Adobe® Reader (a free Adobe Systems application).

Again, the cost increases are also proportionate to the sales activity you expect online.

The bottom line is — every site has a unique budget because every site is a customized product and process. A professional web company will provide a custom budget proposal once they've met with you and determined the scope of your unique site.

What goes into your website DEVELOPMENT budget?

This example is for a $30,000 site.

Task	Cost
Predevelopment costs, including initial meetings to discuss strategy, brand, audience and content Leasing your domain name and setting up your hosting contract	$5,000
Site Requirements Document preparation, including site map blueprints and screen shots for the home page and all sub-pages	$2,500
Project management to oversee the smooth implementation of all phases	$2,500
Keyword research, analysis and recommendations	$2,500
Web-SEO content-writing activities • Conducting research to determine unique value messages • Writing on-page content for each page on the site: sales copy, links, order page, etc. • Writing meta tags for each page on the site	$8,000

Site graphics and development activities • Designing graphics • Coding to build pages, forms, links and other functions	$7,000
Developing photography and other graphics: shooting and preparing product and people images, buying stock images, creating and/or buying illustrations for charts, etc.	$2,500
TOTAL	$30,000

With this budget, we assume your professional web team members will do most of the work. These skilled experts are worth their weight in gold because they'll make your site sizzle and sell!

Once your site is launched, the work doesn't stop there — just like you wouldn't stop advertising your business after 1 press release or 1 direct mail campaign. You'll need to budget for 3 more aspects of a profitable website.

1. Initial Marketing Package

First, to establish your presence on the World Wide Web and help your prospects find your site through various online means, you'll need to invest in a launch marketing package.

It can cost between $5,000 and $20,000 for initial site analysis, domain name analysis, ranking report, linking strategy, in-depth keyword research, a thorough competitive analysis and a comprehensive marketing strategy you can use going forward.

Please note that this is a realistic budget for hiring an extremely skilled, experienced SEO (search engine optimization) expert or team to do the job well for you. There are scam artists in the jungle who will promise you first-page rankings — guaranteed — for very little money.

Important: There's NO possible guarantee of first-page rankings on any search engine. It simply isn't offered on the Internet unless you buy paid AdWords (PPC) campaigns, which we'll discuss in Chapter 6. Therefore, you'll want to steer clear of disreputable companies who say otherwise. (See our OUTSMART 'EM! tip in Chapter 5.)

2. Ongoing Marketing Strategies

Next, to motivate your customers to keep coming back to your site, and to keep adding new customers, you'll need to create and implement various marketing approaches throughout the year. This may include someone to manage your social media campaigns, email newsletters, Pay-Per-Click campaigns, monthly SEO keyphrase adjustments, blogs and more. You'll learn all about these and other useful tactics in Chapters 6 and 7.

Here are some budget guidelines for these various approaches:

- Monthly customized SEO adjustments can run approximately $300 - $1,200. OUTSMART 'EM: Once again, some companies promise first-page ranking for as little as $79 per month. One of C S's customers decided to check it out. When he asked specific questions about what they would do for this price, they hung up on him. 'Nuff said.

- A well-crafted email newsletter will cost $300/month or more, and email "autoresponders" can cost $250 and more each.

- A Pay-Per-Click campaign setup fee is $500-$1,000 plus the cost of clicks and regular monitoring and tweaking for maximum results.

These are just a few examples. Your web team can create a carefully-planned marketing campaign (and budget) designed to reach your target prospects in the most cost-effective and profitable way.

3. **Monthly and Opportunistic Website Maintenance**

For search engines and prospects/customers to keep coming to your site, you need to add fresh content regularly. This may include press releases, new staff member introductions or "featured products of the month," articles, blog posts, new product and service announcements, special events, promotions, upcoming meetings/updated calendar and more.

A web team can help you take care of these things each month, and they'll charge by the hour to do so — usually billed at an hourly rate of $75 to $150 if they're skilled. Some web development companies will offer a maintenance plan on retainer, which means you might arrange to pay $1,000–$5,000 per month for unlimited changes and updates.

You see how this can quickly add up. But remember, your website success is just like your overall success. You need to continue evolving and investing in marketing for steady, sustainable growth. Every one of these ongoing steps will help make your site productive and profitable. It's a commitment to growing your organization's revenue and profits.

Now for the big questions.

How much growth can you expect from your new-and-improved website and online marketing efforts?

What's the return on your investment?

It depends on a number of factors, including the appeal of your products and/or services, the market, how quickly you can identify and reach your target audiences and drive them to your site, your pricing, your offers and many other considerations.

As we mentioned earlier, every pet business, veterinary practice and pet-industry organization and every website is unique. And, since we don't know about your specific products, services, pricing, business structure, brand position or anything else, it's not possible for us to tell you exactly what kind of return you can expect.

However, we can and will tell you what other businesses are experiencing as a result of following website best practices, particularly by adding fresh, helpful content on a regular basis, with additional marketing efforts driving continual engagement.

Here are a number of statistics we found throughout the business community.

* Hubspot customers who practice inbound marketing (of which content is a core element) increase leads by an average of 4.2 times within a few months. Source: http://mashable.com/2011/07/04/how-to-measure-roi-content-marketing-strategy/

* The folks at Best Friends Animal Society in Utah introduced the Invisible Dogs Campaign (http://www.invisibledogs.org/) to bring awareness to forgotten city-shelter dogs. Within a short period after launching a website and Twitter campaign urging people to take action that helps these dogs (adoption, dog walking, etc.), 2,532 people had made the pledge as of this writing.

* Pet food company Royal Canin created a customer loyalty email campaign that generates an astounding average click-through rate (response rate) of 80%. This means that 80% of customers who read their emails click-through to their website to read a full article to take another action. When you consider that 5%-25% click-through rates are considered very successful, the Royal Canin rate is pretty wild. Source: MarketingProfs.com

* The wildly successful pet company Doggles began with a photo posted online. It's now a $3 million company.
  Source: http://www.entrepreneur.com/magazine/entrepreneur/2010/june/ 206722-3.html

In Chapter 14: Measure and Maximize Your Marketing Results, you'll learn how to determine your site's return on investment via your web host's reports and statistics and, of course, your own sales and activity reports.

CHAPTER 4 SUMMARY/ACTION ITEMS:
Wow Them with Your Website

* 3 distinct website areas — Site Architecture, Graphic Design and Content — are equally important for the usability (user-friendliness) and ultimate success of your site.

* Colors, text fonts, numbers of clicks and many other aspects of your page are critical to your site's profitability, because they can either keep your visitors engaged or turn them away.

* The number one rule of successful web content is that it must focus on the customers' needs and offer solutions to meet those needs — what's in it for them.

* "Content is King" because what you SAY on your site is going to attract or repel buyers. Smart marketing content will ensure the best results for your site.

* As you outline your messages for each page, keep in mind that "People aren't surfing the Net anymore, they're searching for very specific solutions."

* Because of this, it's extremely helpful to articulate your Unique Selling Proposition or Unique Solution Proposition to differentiate how your business uniquely solves customer needs.

* People buy benefits, not features. Make sure your strongest and most unique benefits are "above the fold" on your web page so your visitors see immediately how you can help them.

* Plan to include a sign-up incentive for your visitors so you can capture their email addresses and follow up with them often.

* Make it effortless for visitors to buy from you. Don't make them

guess where to go to make purchases — offer clear instructions and an easy checkout process.

* Careful planning, using a Site Map and a Web Creative Brief, will help you avoid the mistakes so many businesses make with their site designs.

* Plan to invest in ongoing marketing efforts to continue growing your traffic and profits.

CHAPTER 4 Additional Notes:

chapter  5

Enlist the Best Team to Support Your Mission

Ensure that your site is alive and running perfectly at all times by finding a host and web team you can trust.

The importance of great hosting

A web host is a server (a special computer) that holds your website's code and images and makes them continually viewable on the Internet.

Think of it as your headquarters in the Internet jungle — the place that serves as your base for your entire online presence. In other words, a host is like a virtual building that holds all the contents of your business or practice on display for customers to see, browse and buy.

Here's how it works.

Let's say you want to visit the Boston Museum of Science's website: www.mos.org.

The diagram at the top of the next page shows how it all happens in the Internet Jungle.

* First, you go to your personal computer and enter the domain name www.mos.org in your web browser software (Internet Explorer, Mozilla Firefox, or Netscape).

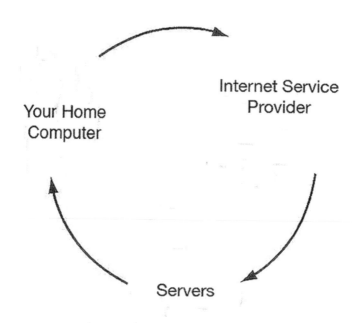

- Next, your browser software connects to your ISP (Internet Service Provider, such as Time Warner/Road Runner, Comcast, CNET, RCN, etc.).

- Your ISP then sends your request to the server that hosts the Boston Museum of Science's website and pulls up their web page (code, images, text, etc.).

- That server sends the Boston Museum of Science website data over the Internet to your computer.

- Your web browser then displays the website on your computer screen.

- This all happens within mere seconds.

Choosing your web host is one of the most important decisions you'll make because you need to make sure your host can keep your site "live."

You need to be able to trust that your site is functioning the way it should at all times! Imagine getting a call in the middle of the night and hearing, **Oh no! Our website is down!**

With the wrong host, you could end up with disastrous downtime, overpay for services, pay for features you don't need, or worse yet, pay more than you expected for functionality that you required but failed to discuss up front.

Let's take a look at price, dependability, features, speed and support you can expect from hosts.

There are three main types of hosts or hosting services:

- **Free Host**
  This is where the old adage, you get what you pay for, applies in a major way. Yes, the host is free, but there's a trade-off: your visitors will be subject to pop-up ads, which are distracting for your customers and a nightmare for your organization.

- **Shared Host**
  This is the most affordable at about $20.00 per month or more. You share the host's server and equipment with many other sites. But, you'll never notice that because from your customer's perspective (and yours), your site will run as a separate entity. Plus, you're given private access to a folder that holds your website.

  Many small-to-midsize businesses share a host and are quite satisfied with the service and reliability. That's what we do at PetCopywriter.com and ATripToTheZoo.com.

- **Dedicated Host**
  In this case, your organization buys its own server dedicated to just your company. Consider this kind of host if you need a lot of file

space and anticipate a large volume of site traffic. A dedicated host can cost $300 to $1,000 per month.

How to find hosts.

To find reliable hosts to consider for your pet-related business, ask people you know and trust because there's a lot of confusion on the web — it's hard to tell who's a legitimate, high-quality host and who isn't.

Your best recommendations for hosts will definitely be from peers and other website marketers you know. Ask them if they like their host and if the service is reliable and responsive.

Another option is to rely on your web team to recommend a host. Or better yet, many web-development companies have their own dedicated host and they offer hosting services to their clients.

It will be well worth your time to do host homework before deciding.

During your search for the right host, you'll find that most web hosting companies offer packages based on the type of site you're building, amount of web space you'll need, amount of traffic your site will have, number of email addresses you require and the type of technology your site requires.

Here are some considerations as you evaluate hosts. Do they ...

- Have enough data storage space for your site? (Enough disk space to hold your pages, images, sound clips, etc.)

- Have enough data transfer (bandwidth)? This is the data transfer activity your contract supports for what's going back and forth between your site and your customers (forms, downloads, play video, etc.). "Bandwidth" is the total of all activity related to your site in a given month. Each hosting contract gives you a certain amount of gigabytes each month. If you go over that amount, you will be upgraded to a higher-level plan, which costs more.

- Offer individual sign-in to upload your website? Will they assign you a unique user ID and password for your site?

- Deliver 24/7 "uptime?" Your site should be up and running at least 99.9% of the time. (When the server is down, your website is down.)

- Provide the number of email accounts (POP3 email accounts) you'll need as you grow?

- Offer email aliases, forwarding and autoresponder capabilities? These allow you to set up names @yourdomain.com that forward to a different email account or to automatically respond to incoming emails while you're out of the office.

- Provide access to traffic log reports on your visitor traffic activities?

- Offer virus and spam protection? (What kind? Can they show proof?)

- Offer robust backup services? The hosting company should be backing up all your website files at least every 24 hours (ecommerce sites even more often!).

- Have outstanding technical support available? Do they provide skilled and accessible support via phone, online or email? Is the phone support live or automated?

- Give you access to site management tools (via a control panel) so you can check billing information or check disk space and band width consumption?

- Operate secure and reliable facilities? Do they ensure fast operation and backup power/generator in case of power outages, etc.?

* Provide a secure server to process credit-card transactions?

IMPORTANT POINTER

Great customer service is critical in a hosting company.

Ask about customer support availability and responsiveness.

1. Besides support hours, how long will you be placed on hold before someone can answer your questions?

2. Ask about the skills of the support staff. Can the person who answers the phone really answer your questions and resolve your issue?

3. What happens during a disaster, such as power outages, floods or fires? Look for guaranteed uptime.

4. Ask for references. Call the references and ask about their experiences with the hosting company.

A final note about your hosting contract:

Don't just shop for hosting services by price or your website may suffer. Examine the contract and make sure the host can provide everything you need. And of course, monitor your host bill. As your site grows, so will your traffic, and you may be required to pay a larger fee.

It pays to address these matters up front, before you sign a contract.

Now, let's look at the other important members of your web team.

Work with a Great Web Team

Find the team you can trust to create your high-quality, profitable site.

As we've mentioned before, creating a successful website is a job for the pros.

Would you let your nephew Johnny or a high-school neighbor do your taxes or negotiate the sale of your home? Or, would you let a first-year college student prescribe medications to your horse?

"No way!" you say. Then why trust your website investment to a novice?

To ensure your best chance at online success, you need to find the best people you can afford; people who have experience in creating profit-generating websites.

As with any professional service, you get what you pay for. If you do all your homework (by following this guide), and you find a great team of web professionals, your site's new pages or updates will be done right THE FIRST TIME and launched sooner than if you go with an inexperienced team.

So Who's Who in Website Development?

Some or all of the following roles must be included in your web team for maximum results. Often, one person can fill many of these roles, so you may only need 3 individuals: a designer, a programmer/developer, and a copywriter. Let's look at each role.

Project Manager — This is your trusted liaison for the entire web team and the person who:
- Directs the building of the website project
- Meets with the client (you) to outline goals, objectives and tasks
- Presents the project proposal and Site Requirements Document
- Establishes the web team's "To-Do" list and timeline

* Keeps everyone on the web team informed and on schedule
* Reviews progress with you
* Manages the team's roles, responsibilities and ability to meet deadlines
* Is a task master with attention to detail

Web Designer — This professional is a graphic artist who designs the look and feel of your site, using web design expertise and skills to:

* Create appropriate visuals to support the functions and readability of your site
* Create page layouts that support usability
* Choose user-friendly colors, fonts and images
* Apply your brand to the website design
* Place all text and graphic elements in a user-friendly manner, guiding users to the information they need

Web Developer/Programmer — This advanced web designer:

* Analyzes your site elements and needs and develops a plan for maximum functionality
* Creates your site map and page "wireframe" outlines (working with others)
* Oversees the programming and testing of your site
* Merges the graphic design and coding to create the actual site
* Writes custom code when needed
* Tests the site's functionality in all browser versions and types

Information Architect — This professional content planner:

* Understands "the art and science of organizing and labeling websites, intranets, online communities and software to support usability and findability"*
* Translates your various information sections into a logical flow
* Maps out where information will be located on each page
* Provides wireframe documents that clearly indicate the navigation, content sections and links

*Information Architecture Institute definition.

Web-SEO Content Writer — This professional is a Certified SEO Copywriter or advanced marketing copywriter who:

- Has expertise in writing online sales copy and has written dozens of successful sites
- Understands usability and the user experience
- Understands how to research and weave in relevant keyphrases in an ethical manner
- Writes to capture your prospects' attention quickly with clear, persuasive sales copy
- Writes benefit messages that are customer-focused
- Writes clear calls-to-action that drive responses
- Ensures that your company's unique offerings stand out immediately
- Writes all the SEO meta tags (explained in Chapters 4 and 6)
- Knows how to write for web pages, enewsletters, landing pages, blog posts, emails and other ongoing content marketing strategies

This role is different from a technical SEO Expert. Please see below.

Webmaster — This technically-gifted website administrator is responsible for:

- Maintaining a site
- Keeping it up-to-date with fresh content and new pictures
- Testing links to ensure the site pages are connected properly
- Helping to build the site
- Creating and updating pages

Ecommerce Specialist — This skilled professional has expertise in:

- Connecting the front-end/site storefront to the back-end/shopping cart
- Connecting to credit-card processing software to set up secure payments online
- Placing products for sale in ways that match online shopping patterns
- Makes recommendations that can strengthen how your products are featured

Usability Expert — This valued specialist:

- Studies global usability issues
- Analyzes your site elements and needs and develops a plan for maximum functionality
- Ensures that your site follows the usability best practices
- Creates your site map and page outlines (working with others)

Search Engine Optimization (SEO) Expert — This highly analytical and detail-oriented individual:

- Markets websites in search engines and follows the ever-changing search engine rules and algorithms
- Creates your site map and page outlines (working with others)
- Understands how to drive traffic to a website in an ethical manner
- Provides file names, image names, keyword research and placement
- Develops search marketing strategies and solutions

This role works in conjunction with an SEO Copywriter as noted previously.

Social Media, New Media Strategist — This marketing expert:

- Follows and uses social media trends and best practices for Facebook, LinkedIn, Twitter and other social sites.
- Follows and uses new media trends and best practices for viral marketing tools such as video, blogging, and audio, as well as online teaching/marketing tools such as webinars, teleconferences, ebooks and white papers.
- Develops social media and new media marketing plans for clients, selecting and implementing strategic paths through the new media landscape. In other words, clients can't do everything all at once, so this professional helps clients select the best approaches for each type of website and company.

Photographer and/or Videographer — A skilled web photographer knows:

- Proper lighting
- Angles that work best on the web to show dimension and depth
- File size requirements
- File management (where photos are stored and managed)
- Ideal pixel sizes for viewing and loading

- Photo enhancement for the web, such as cropping, shading, etc.
- Video editing and file formats for the web

NOTE: Be careful when using stock images. We recently attended a veterinary trade show where at least 6 different companies used the exact same stock photo of a female vet holding a cat. This confuses the heck out of customers: which company is which? They all look the same. We highly recommend investing in a professional photographer to take at least a few original images for your business brand, so you don't get lost in all that "sameness."

Other Online Marketing Experts — You may also engage these professionals for assistance. We explain their work in Chapter 10:
- PPC firms: Professionals who run your paid search marketing campaigns
- Link-building firms: Professionals who find excellent websites for your organization to place links with

Now that you know each role in your web development team, it's time to find reputable web companies to interview for the job of creating your site.

To find a great company or savvy expert, ask a few colleagues you know who have a site that really works. (If you're lucky, you know someone personally who has a great website!) It's always best to go with companies that come with the approval of a friend or colleague.

In addition, we can steer you to reputable, reliable web development companies to consider. Each of them have experience with pet businesses and/or veterinary practices. **(Be sure to check the Resources section in the back of this book to see if these vendors have a special offer for you.)**

Black Dog Studios www.BlackDogDev.com
Idextrus www.Idextrus.com
Image Works www.imagewks.com/

LifeLearn WebDVM4 (specifically for veterinary practices)
www.lifelearn.com/for-veterinary-teams/

You can also search the Internet for web development companies in your area. Let's say you're located in Chicago. You can use the keywords: "web developers chicago." We tried this and found a dozen web companies listed on the first ranking page in Google.

Once you've created a list of web development companies in your region, it's time to find the best one for your site.

So, how can you tell the good hires from the risky hires?

By using the following questionnaire. But, first...

OUTSMART 'EM!
Just like in the animal world, predators are lurking in the online marketing world.

As a reader of this guide, you can outsmart 'em because we're giving you the inside scoop on how these predators operate.

Here's an all-too-common story from a company that manufactures and sells retail products in the pet industry.

"We were looking for SEO marketing and responded to a local company who told us we didn't have to sign a contract. We were told we could just go by the month, and we could cancel at any time without penalties.

I usually just get rid of someone calling about marketing because I assume they're probably not going to do us any good. But 'David' was so nice, and spent so much time with us, we said we'd try it for a month since we didn't have to sign a contract. David assured us over and over that we could opt out at any time.

David called every day and was so nice that we'd never think he was trapping us into a $1,300 payment for the next month. He acted like he really cared.

As the time approached to decide if we wanted to sign up for another month, we told David several times we just didn't have the money. David then told us he had a chance to include us in a Facebook blast that would go out to millions of people and this was a great opportunity to build social media presence.

By that time, we both trusted David, but we told him that if we didn't see anything from the blast, we wouldn't be able to go on for another month. He always reassured us that if we didn't see an improvement in sales, we could quit at any time.

He said that he was sending something over for us to see about the blast so, while we were on the phone, he said just to say, 'I accept' so they could get us signed up for the blast going out that day.

I can't tell you how shocked I was to see that they had taken $1,300 out of our account. When I called David, he said that he would go right to the office and take care of it. After repeated calls and no luck, he finally wrote me an email to tell me what was going on.

Here's exactly what he wrote:

I'm about 5 minutes from being done. I had no idea what our billing department did, let me walk in and see what happened after I get off the phone. I would never do that, it just re-occurs, and I send over a cancellation in the database. I'm figuring 5 more minutes with this guy, then I will walk in over and find out what happened. Then call.

Of course, when we finally talked to David, he reassured us that the money would be refunded to us. After that, he was unavailable.

Then, I talked to the office and got a woman that basically screamed at me for about 10 minutes until I finally understood that there had been an attachment to the email from David and they were waiting for me to sign it. The blast was ready to go and they were waiting for me. The attachment was their terms of agreement, and I hadn't noticed it before. David was talking so much and pressing me to not miss the blast that I was oblivious. I'm really not that stupid and think that I'm pretty leery of anyone selling me something on the Internet... but the key here was that I trusted David.

We tried to dispute it with our bank, but guess what — they were armed with tricky evidence that their lawyers made into a big deal. For instance, I was asked to write a testimonial for David's company when he seemed to be working so hard for us. And to tell the truth, since David had almost become a friend, I did write one.

Ultimately, they won and kept our money.

We hope we can spare anyone else this pain by telling our story."
— Jeanne and Krystal, Pet Business Owners

The Web Team Interview Questionnaire
Hire the best crew you can afford

You'll also find this sheet in the Appendix section.

You wouldn't leave your dog with a boarding service without checking out the setting and the crew who will be taking care of him. The same applies to your web development team.

To get a true sense of what a professional web team can do for you, use these interview questions when you meet with the various candidates:

- What are your credentials?

- What is your site domain? (Take a look at the candidate's site to see if it follows the best practices we've outlined in Chapter 4.)

- What are your technical capabilities?

- What skills and training do you have?

- Can you provide samples of your work — sites that are optimized, profitable and successful?

- Do you have any before/after screen shots, case studies, or other proof of your work results?

- Can you describe your web development process?

- Can you explain your process and its phases in non-technical terms so I can understand and make smart decisions?

- What's the average budget range you work with?

- Will you turn over ownership of all graphics created for my site?

- Would you please provide references from at least 3 satisfied clients?

Use the answers to these questions to determine if the person or team is worth working with or asking for a detailed proposal.

IMPORTANT POINTER

Tips for screening and hiring a great web team:

* Plan to interview 2 or 3 web companies for an informed comparison.

* Schedule an initial consultation with each team or representative (this consultation should be free).

* Gather the information you've created through this guide to show them what kind of site you need and want. Also show them examples of your brand elements, such as your logo, fonts, colors, ads, business card, brochure and others.

* Give them a list of sites you like and don't like, and tell them why.

* Ask them the interview questions we've provided and ask to see samples of their work. Also, ask for proof of their skills: their client websites and their own, plus case studies and before/after screen shots.

* If you like what you find during the interview/consultation, ask them for a proposal in writing, which usually includes a Site Requirements Document (site blueprints, screen shots, cost, etc., of what the team will do for you). NOTE: A reputable/experienced firm will require a payment for this phase because of the work that's involved, which is fair.

That's it! The 2 or 3 teams should respond by presenting you with terrific proposals, and you should be able to make a comfortable choice.

CHAPTER 5 SUMMARY/ACTION ITEMS:
Enlist the Best Team to Support Your Mission

* A web host is a server (a special computer) that serves as the online "building" that houses your website and makes it continually viewable on the Internet.

* Choosing a reliable web host is important for keeping your site "live" at all times and functioning the way you expect.

* A shared host is the most affordable way to go unless you're a larger business and need tons of storage and functionality. Many organizations are quite satisfied with shared host service and reliability.

* There are a lot of unreliable hosts out there who will promise you the moon. To find reliable hosts you can trust, ask other marketers you know who are happy with their sites.

* Ask lots of questions when talking with various hosts, especially regarding customer service. Always examine a host contract before you sign it, so there are no surprises down the road when you need more space or added services.

* To ensure your best chance at online success, you need to find the best people you can afford; people who have experience in creating profit-generating websites.

* To find a great web development company, ask colleagues you know who have profitable sites. You can also search the Internet for web development companies in your area.

* Interview 2 or 3 firms to determine which one is the best for your project. To make sure you ask everything you need to know, just use the interview questions we've provided. Most important, be sure to ask for samples of their work!

- These teams should provide you with a written proposal that includes blueprints and screen shots of what they'll do for you.

- Don't worry about all the little details. A great web team will walk you through the process and help you with the aspects that need your attention.

CHAPTER 5 Additional Notes:

PART III

Cultivate profitable relationships using today's best marketing tools.

Aww. So much love and trust here. *The relationship between this dog and cat is clearly solid, with complete trust and happiness. This is the kind of relationship that businesses DREAM of — a relationship where customers become loyal, satisfied fans for life. It takes time and effort to build these relationships, but every day, by taking a "customer-first" approach, you can get closer and continually grow. That's what this section is about. (Best Buds photo captured by Pam Foster's son Ben Tardiff)*

Now that your website is solid and you've included search engine optimization (SEO) strategies to bring more traffic to your site… it's time to add a variety of marketing ingredients to expand your reach and enjoy steady growth.

In this section, you'll discover the most popular marketing options that work wonders today… and how to choose and use them successfully for your specific mission.

Try not to get overwhelmed by this section! The best way to begin is this:

1. Become familiar with the various marketing tools and techniques. They're all optional!

2. Choose just 1 or 2 approaches to start with. Give them a 100% effort and you'll become more comfortable with them. You'll also see encouraging results that make it worth your time and energy.

3. Add another marketing approach when you're ready.

4. Slowly build your arsenal throughout the next 12 months.

5. Be sure to track how each effort is doing, so you can adjust and drive even bigger results.

Think tortoise, not hare. Slow and steady wins the race in general, although you may find that some of these methods give you a nice jump-start.

Ready? Let's go…

Attract a Stampede of Eager Prospects with SEO (Search Engine Optimization)

Bring a herd of eager prospects to your website and physical location (if applicable) via Google, Bing and other search engines.

91% of U.S. adults use a search engine to find information. (Pew Internet) SEO refers to the practice of enhancing the words (content), code (behind-the-scenes programming) and other technical elements of your website so it will rank high in the search engines such as Google, Bing and Yahoo!. With professional assistance, SEO can help boost your online traffic in a huge way because more prospects find you in search engines.

In case you're not sure how search engines work, allow us to explain. A search engine is a website that primarily functions as a clearinghouse for gathering and reporting information available on the Internet or a portion of the Internet. People type keywords or "queries" into these search sites to find what they're looking for.

At the moment, the top five search engines are Google, YouTube (searching for videos), Bing, Yahoo! and Ask.

Source: http://www.ebizma.com/articles/search-engines

A web crawler (also known as a web spider or web robot/'bot) is the technology that browses the World Wide Web in a methodical, automated manner, collecting the information found on visited pages. This includes the content visitors see ON a web page as well as the content included behind-the-scenes in programming code. The crawlers store this information for later processing by search engines.

What happens when a user types keywords into a search engine? Here's a super-simplified explanation of a highly technical process:

* The whole process comes together when a search engine "indexes" web pages that are relevant to those keywords, and then provides web page rankings (search results) based on what was found at that moment in time.

* The algorithms used by these sites are extremely complex, and they change frequently to keep hackers from dominating the results. This also ensures that keyword results are always fresh and relevant to searchers.

Here's what we mean by keywords.

If you're looking for a pet ID tag featuring St. Francis of Assisi, the patron saint of animals, you'll probably go to the Google search engine and type in the keyword phrases (also known as keyphrases): "st francis pet ID tag" or "st francis dog tag" or something similar. These keyphrases are very likely to be used by other people looking for St. Francis ID tags. So, the companies that sell St. Francis tags, such as this one, will also likely use these keyphrases:

St. Francis Pet ID Tag, St. ✅
www.stfrancispetmedals.com/
A **St. Francis Pet ID Tag** from St. Francis Pet Medals makes a divine gift for pets and pet lovers. Engraved brass or silver-plate for dog, cat, horse.

IMPORTANT POINTER

Know your keywords to drive more traffic to your site.

The foundation of successful SEO is in knowing the keywords your prospects use in Google and other search engines to find solutions to their needs.

Let's say this again because it's so important:

The foundation of successful SEO is in knowing THE KEYWORDS your prospects use in search engines to find solutions to their needs.

- First, when we talk about keywords, we actually mean keyphrases (made up of 3 to 5 keywords). People rarely search for something using a single word anymore. Plus, the word "dog" alone will not be useful to you. There are too many competing web pages that use the word "dog." So, although the web industry calls them keywords, think of phrases people may use to find what you offer, such as "dog emergency tips," "[city] dog parks," and "dog groomers in [city]."

- A profitable website is one that's "keyword rich," meaning it revolves around carefully-chosen and strategically-placed keywords within the content and coding.

- Keywords are big business! Your competition could race ahead of you if they use your keywords more effectively than you do.

- Carefully select keywords by truly understanding the words used by your desired audience. (This goes back to knowing your target audience and what they seek. You may want to revisit Chapter 3 when thinking about which keywords are best for your web pages.)

- Each page should focus on its own keywords used in an ethical manner that weaves them into clear messages for your visitors.

For example, if a prospect is looking for Maine coon cat products and gifts, and that's what you offer, you'll want to make sure your web pages include the specific keyphrases, "Maine coon cat gifts," "Maine coon cat books."

How do we know which keywords are best for your web pages? Online research tools, such as the free Google AdWords Keyword Tool, show you which keywords (phrases) people are using to find various topics related to your organization.

For example, if you type the words "Maine coon cat" in the Keyword Tool, you'll see a list of words that include gift-related phrases like these:

maine coon cat photos
maine coon cat gifts (and gift)
maine coon cat art
maine coon cat calendar
maine coon cat books

These lists give a clue as to which keywords to feature on your web pages.

9 Specific Steps to Finding the Best Keywords for Your Site

1. **Make a list of all the keywords you can think of for each web page or topic.** Again, they're actually groups of phrases, but the industry calls them keywords to simplify the discussion. 3- to 5-word combinations, such as "maine coon cat gifts" are best. This is known as a "long-tail" keyword phrase, meaning longer phrases are more specific to what the searcher is looking for. Fewer people may use these long-tail phrases, but those who do are motivated individuals who will be delighted to find your website!

2. **Put yourself in your customers' shoes as you consider keywords.** You can do this by interviewing customers, doing informal email surveys, or even conducting formal surveys online via MyEmma. com, SurveyMonkey.com and other online survey providers.

3. **Check out your website's traffic reports.** If you already have a web site, you can get keywords from your own traffic logs (from your hosting company or Google Analytics data). You'll find more information on this in Chapter 14: Measure and Maximize Your Marketing Results.

4. **Check out your competition to discover the keywords they're targeting.** Enter your keywords and see what pages come up. Take a look at how their descriptions are written, as shown below.

   Also, on their sites, go to the top menu of your Internet screen and select "View," then "Source" (Internet Explorer) or "View," then "Page Source" (Mozilla Firefox) to look at the source codes — showing their "meta keywords" (depending on how the site is coded). We show you what this looks like in a couple of pages further along.

   Maine Coon Cat Lover T-Shirt and **Gift** Shop
   www.cafepress.com/mainecooncats
   Maine Coons Cat gifts for everyone. T-shirts and gift items for cat lovers. Featuring the gentle giant of the cat world, the Maine Coon Cat.

   Maine Coon Cat Gifts
   www.animalden.com › Cats
   Maine Coon Cat Gifts, Products & Merchandise for all Maine Coon Cat lovers. A world of great items like Calendars, T-shirts, Signs, Plush & Stuffed Animals, ...

   Maine Coon Cat Gifts - Zazzle
   www.zazzle.com/maine+coon+cat+gifts
   60+ items – Choose your favorite **maine coon cat gift** from thousands of ...
   $3.35   **Maine Coon Cat** Face Key Ring Keychains   see on 3 styles or 3 ...
   $14.45   **Maine Coon Cat** Mug Rustic   see on 7 styles

   Maine Coon Cat Lover Gifts
   www.maine-coon-cat-nation.com/cat-lover-gifts.html
   We are so excited to offer these unique and exclusive designs! Whatever your fancy, you'll find **Maine Coon cat** lover **gifts** here!

5. **Cover all keyword variations.** Keep in mind that people may use plurals or other words or phrases relevant to your web pages. The free Google AdWords Keyword Tool provides keyword synonyms so you can find terms you may not have considered.

6. **Be descriptive.** Add descriptive terms to your keyword considerations, such as "low cost," "affordable," "how to," "discount," "free," etc.

7. **Use action words.** Think of what your customers are trying to do — buy, find, purchase, define, shop, etc.

8. **Target local markets if that's relevant.** If your dog daycare clinic is in Beaufort, your keywords should include "Beaufort dog," "Beaufort dog daycare," etc.

9. **Use online keyword research tools.** There are a number of companies offering keyword research and rankings. Google AdWords Keyword Tool is free but limited. www.Wordtracker.com, www.KeywordDiscovery.com and others offer more robust information for a fee. (Tip: They may have a free trial available as well.)

One more thing. Please keep in mind that there are many different ways to search for something, so your business may have many different keywords associated with it, depending on your target audience's perspective.

Take "maine coon cat," again for example. As we noted, the first relevant keywords you find might be any of the following:
* maine coon cat photos
* maine coon cat gifts (and gift)
* maine coon cat art
* Etc.

But, you may also find, as we did, additional keywords in Google that don't use the word "cat":
* maine coon kittens
* maine coon kitten gifts

The point is — the most relevant keywords for your prospects may not be the most obvious at first, or they may be a combination of several variations. This is important to remember as you create your list of key-words to research.

You'll find a keyword research worksheet in the Appendix.

After determining the most relevant keywords for your business, the next step in SEO is to make sure your TOP keywords are placed properly throughout your site's content.

Your web team's content writer and programmer will make sure the top 2 or 3 unique keywords (phrases) for each web page are woven into the following key areas:

* **Page headers, also known as headlines.** Don't waste valuable space with "Welcome to our home page" in the header!

  Ideally, headlines should be written using your keywords as part of a big, bold promise that benefits the visitor. For example, using the example keyword of "dog park equipment" a headline might be:

  > **The first full line of dog park equipment specifically designed for public park use**

  (This is the headline on the home page of www.Dog-On-It-Parks.com)

* **Body text subheads, links, captions, and bold areas.** Most sites, with the exception of certain sites such as sales letter landing pages or very robust research or library pages, should contain at least 250-500 words of visible text on each page. Other body copy tips include:

  * Place special emphasis on your carefully-chosen keywords, weaving them into natural-sounding narrative text, subheads, bullets, callouts and other text elements. This includes "Alt tags"— the

captions for your pictures and other images, as well as link content, such as articles or reports.

- Make sure pages are written to attract prospects and search engines alike. This means the messages are clear, appealing, persuasive and solution-focused... and they weave in the top keyphrases that are relevant for that web page.

- After the home page, sub-pages on your site should focus on specific keywords for each page. For example, a local dog-services site may have unique pages featuring daycare, boarding, grooming, walking, etc. A grooming page would have different keywords than a page featuring dog-walking services.

- **Domain names (web addresses).** If possible, make keywords a part of your domain name and sub-page domain names, such as "www.yourstore.com/waterproofdogjackets."

So, now you know about adding your top 2 or 3 keywords to the web page copy your visitors will be reading. Sounds simple, right? Well... read on.

Adding relevant keyphrases to your visible "on-page" web content is just one part of "optimizing" your web content for search engines.

The other part, and this is equally important, is making sure every page of your site includes **the top 2 or 3 most relevant keyphrases** in your site's behind-the-scenes "meta tags" (code) as we mentioned in Chapter 4's usability guidelines.

Meta tags are important because search engines read and often display them in search results.

We'll repeat them here and show you what they look like in the "View Source" code of a website:

* **Page Title tag** with keywords/keyphrases (70 characters/spaces maximum; real sentences are best: <title>title goes here </title>).

This is the most critical location for your keywords!

Not only does the Page Title appear at the very top of your website page, above your "creative banner" as shown below — but it's the first part of your web page's listing in search results, such as your Google results, and can entice people to click-through.

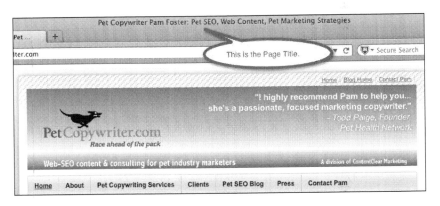

Search engines consider the keywords found in the Page Title as extremely important, so be sure to place your top keywords here if possible!

* **Meta Description** using keywords/keyphrases in an inviting, complete sentence or two (this may be displayed in Google's search results; limit to 150 characters/spaces). Here's an example using the search engine keywords "leather dog collars." It's the first website listed in Google for that phrase:

```
<title>Leerburg | Leather Dog Leashes</title>
<!-- InstanceEndEditable -->
<meta http-equiv="Content-Type" content="text/html; charset=iso-8859-1" />
<!-- InstanceBeginEditable name="head" -->
<META NAME="Keywords" CONTENT="Leash, Leather, Dog, Handmade, Amish, Leerburg, Puppy">
<META NAME="Description" CONTENT="Leerburg leather dog leashes are the finest quality lead you c
Amish from soft Latigo leather. You will not find a better dog leash anywhere! ">
```

- **Meta keywords** (Up to 10 keyword phrases, starting the top 2 or 3 phrases you'll feature in your content.)

- **Alt tags** with keywords/keyphrases (for charts, photos and other graphics that aren't text)

In a nutshell, your SEO plan will include:

- Analyzing your website to make sure the navigation and content are easy to read (for web crawlers/spiders and indexes)

- Reviewing your competition — scrutinizing their search engine rankings and the keywords they use in their sites

- Choosing the most relevant keywords your target prospects and customers are using

- Optimizing page content (on-page sales copy) and the HTML code behind the scenes (off-page meta tags)

- Staying up-to-date with monthly search engine algorithm changes

Of course, you won't be doing this alone. Your web copywriter and team will manage as little or as much of this as you wish. We just wanted to help you become more SEO-savvy so you know what your web copywriter is doing and why.

Before we move on to the next online marketing strategy, we have a few OUTSMART 'EM! tips for you regarding SEO.

1. **Meta Tags: Myth vs. Fact.**

   Myth: Meta tags no longer propel your web page to the top of the search engines.

Fact: The truth is — Certain meta tags (page title and description) are displayed in search results, and search engines DO view them. In addition, your prospects will read them to decide whether or not to click-through to your website… or another site. That's why meta tags are still critical, as you'll see here when we Googled the keyphrase "dog walker rhode island":

Professional **Dog Walker Pet** Sitter North Kingstown, RI. NK ... ⑦
Looking for reliable **dog-walking** and **pet**-sitting services in the North Kingstown, **Rhode Island** area? If you're concerned about your **dog's** well being while you ...
nkdogwalking.com/index.html - Cached

2. Search Engine Submissions: Just Say No.

Back in the early days of search engines, everyone needed to submit their website domain names and descriptions as a way of letting the search engines know that their sites and individual pages existed.

This is no longer the case. In fact, most search engines prefer to find you organically, or naturally, through their own web crawlers and stored information.

Unfortunately, there are hundreds of companies that will offer to submit your website pages for a fee so you'll "be guaranteed to rank at the top of every search engine for listings in your business category!"

Don't buy into it — literally! It's just not prudent to spend your money chasing down the dream of "buying" organic (non-sponsored) search engine rankings. It doesn't work for the following three reasons:

* Search engines never guarantee that your site will be indexed, even if you pay them.

- Google, Bing, Yahoo! and MSN don't even let you buy submissions — they prefer to find you via their own spiders.

- Companies that promise you top rankings are usually scam artists that just want your money. Only PAID search marketing campaigns will put your web pages on top in the "sponsored links" sections of search results.

Therefore, please do not take the bait and pay someone to submit your site to search engines. You'll be throwing your money away. (See OUTSMART 'EM! In Chapter 5.)

3. **Google's "Panda Update" has changed everything.**

Google has clamped down hard on websites that simply use "poor-quality articles stuffed with keywords" or even duplicate content found on other websites. The Google intent is that they will only rank "quality" websites, with original, useful content that actually helps the person seeking solutions. Google rewards websites that offer something unique and highly relevant.

This means if you manage an online store/ecommerce website and you're using the manufacturer's content for each product you carry… we're afraid your online store's content is considered a duplicate and it might be invisible to search engines. You're missing out on oodles of traffic from potential customers.

Find ways to offer *original* content on your website so you can attract more customers via SEO. **This means you need to revise each of the manufacturers' product descriptions with your own spin.**

For example, if your online pet supply store includes a particular line of products because they're eco-friendly and they reflect your commitment to green products — say so! Tell your visitors why the products are favored by you and treasured by your customers. Make a point to add your own brand voice to the copy. No one has the same brand voice as you, so this will help make your content unique. Customer reviews can also help, but if you're just starting to offer those, start revising the product descriptions ASAP.

Also, to stay current in search results, you need to find a way to add fresh, original and highly-relevant content to your site each week.

This is because your competition is likely to be doing this… and if you don't keep up, you'll fall behind.

One way to solve this is by including an active blog on your website (see Chapter 7). You'll be delighted and amazed at the search-engine traffic power of writing helpful blog posts. We recently started helping a pet-industry client add blog posts each week, and suddenly after 6 posts or so, the client's site is turning up on top of Google's page one for the keywords we targeted. These blog posts are getting attention and driving site visits — all with just a few posts for starters.

4. **Be aware that there are nasty tricksters out there.**

Sadly, unscrupulous web hackers try to manipulate the search engines through a variety of measures. These "black hat SEO" marauders are part of the group discussed in OUTSMART 'EM! in Chapter 5, and here are some of the scammy practices they follow:

*   Spamdexing, which means stuffing or repeating keywords over and over on a web page. Search engines do not allow this practice — they'll actually boot you out of their rankings if they find spammed pages. And, visitors will ditch your site instantly when they recognize this practice.

- Invisible or semi-invisible ghosted text, which users can't see, but search engines pick up.

- Doorway pages, where they create one page the users see and then other pages designed just for search engines.

- "Link buying," which means the practice of buying inbound links from disreputable firms... all promising to boost SEO. (This is different from legitimate Link Building services we discuss in Chapter 10.)

- Bogus "phishing" SEO providers who email you with a message starting, "Dear Sir or Madam" and continue with a message full of typos and generic promises of top rankings. Yikes.

If you talk with a web "professional" who suggests any of these tricks, run. And, don't look back. The results of these illegal actions can cause your site to be blacklisted from search engines and rarely indexed again.

 IMPORTANT POINTER

SEO takes time to spring into action, and there are no guarantees.

Web crawlers collect website information every 3 to 8 weeks, or even sooner with certain types of content such as blog posts. A brand-new site may take even longer to process. On top of this, each search engine has its own pace for indexing sites and pages.

Therefore, the initial SEO tactics performed on your site may not deliver results instantly. Just know that you will see an improvement over time as the system kicks in. The only way to have faster results is to pay for your results (through non-organic measures such as Pay-Per-Click advertising), which we explain in Chapter 10.

Finally, nobody can guarantee top results for organic search rankings.

There are several factors — personalization, localization, competition, social media and many others — that can affect one person's search results over another's. For example, if you're in Brooklyn and your colleague is in LA, the search results are sure to be different.

So never, ever believe anyone who promises you top rankings in organic search results. Again, the only sure results are paid ads (sponsored links), which we talk about in Chapter 10.

CHAPTER 6 SUMMARY/ACTION ITEMS:
Attract a Stampede with Search Engine Optimization (SEO)

- The foundation of successful SEO is in knowing the keywords your prospects use in search engines to find solutions to their needs.

- You can use online tools, such as the free Google AdWords Keyword Tool, to find out which keywords people are using.

- After determining the most relevant keywords for your business, the next step in SEO is to make sure your TOP keywords are placed properly throughout your site, primarily in headlines; body text sub-heads, links, captions, and bold areas; and domain names.

- Meta tags are very important because search engines often display them in search results, and people decide to click-through to your site based on what those tags say.

- Your Page Title Tags are the most critical because people often click on those first in search engine results.

- SEO takes time to spring into action, and there are no guarantees.

- Never believe anyone who promises you top rankings in organic search results. The only sure results are paid ads (sponsored links), which we talk about in Chapter 10.

CHAPTER 6 Additional Notes:

Connect with Fans Through Social Media (Online Networking)

Lead fans and followers to you with a clever approach to Facebook, Twitter, YouTube/video, blogs and more.

When you connect one-on-one with your prospects in the various social networks, you can easily turn them into loyal fans… and buying customers.

It's clear that social media is strong and growing as a place where many of your target prospects and ideal customers are congregating with like-minded people, sharing things they like (and don't like), and engaging with pet-related brands that give them strong reasons to engage.

Keep in mind that social media started as free discussion boards where people could discuss and share interests, hobbies, lifestyles, events, pop culture, news events and more. Wikipedia refers to social media as "user-generated content (UGC) or consumer-generated media (CGM)." This means the consumers rule the content, NOT the advertisers. It's very personal.

Facebook, Twitter and other popular social networking sites are gaining thousands if not millions of members each week. And, pet businesses and veterinary practices are finding these sites extremely useful for reaching out to people who love dogs, cats, horses and other animals. More on that in a moment.

First, we'd like to make it clear that when we discuss social media (the platforms) and social networking (the act of connecting) in this guide, we're mainly talking about today's big 4 social venues known to drive business from consumers: Facebook, Twitter, YouTube and Blogging. There are many other social networks that may benefit you — such as Google+ and Pinterest— but these are the big 4 at the moment when it comes to audience size, participation and potential traffic to your website.

❧ Facebook

In May 2013, Facebook reached 1.11 billion members. And, millions upon millions of those people LOVE pets. They love talking about pets, sharing funny photos and videos, discovering new products and services, talking with pet folks and much more. Check out Jett and Monkey's Dog Shoppe Facebook page here to see what we mean.

Some have even set up Facebook pages for their pets — including Facebook founder Mark Zuckerberg's page for Beast, his dog.
It's easy to maintain a fan-friendly Facebook page for your pet business or veterinary practice, as we explain in a moment.

Twitter

Twitter's promise is simply this: "Follow your interests, with instant updates from your friends, industry experts, favorites celebrities and what's happening around the world." In 140 characters or fewer, people tweet, share, link and drive all kinds of conversations that can end up leading to business for savvy marketers.

In August 2013, Twitter reached over 500 million tweets a day. And, if you look at the demographics, you'll find there's a lot of potential business for you there. The male/female ratio is split nearly evenly, the majority of users are between 26 and 44 years of age, 25% of members follow a brand, and of those… 67% will purchase that brand.

Source: http://www.marketinggum.com/twitter-statistics-2011-updated-stats/

Here's a snapshot of the Cesar Millan's Twitter page. Whether you're a fan of him or not, you may be impressed to see that he has more than 539,171 followers as of this writing!

* **YouTube**

Online video clips are extremely useful marketing tools when presented properly. They can bring your pet business or veterinary practice to life and be fantastic sales-drivers by giving people a glimpse of what you offer, providing a credible testimonial, showing someone how to do something or introducing yourself to customers, etc.

When you post videos on your own website, you can also post them on your organization's YouTube channel. This is an exciting way to reach thousands of people, because pet fans flock to YouTube to find great videos. Out of the millions of YouTube videos posted in 2011, the second most popular video was a funny dog video called The Ultimate Dog Tease.

Every day, people are looking for entertaining or informative pet videos to watch. Plus, they leave comments on your YouTube page and share the links, building even more and more traffic to your video, your website and your business!

Check out the Manchester West Veterinary Hospital's "Pet Tips-Thanksgiving Dangers" YouTube video below to see what we mean: www.youtube.com/watch?v=FDHAHs8WXZU

Blogging

As you know, blogs, or weblogs, are everywhere! They allow anyone to post frequent, sequential online essays of thoughts, tips, reviews and web links.

A pet business or veterinary practice blog may include commentary about trends in pet care, new pet products and amazing pet stories, or post questions and answers or even contest invitations. Plus, pet business blog writers and editors often invite readers to respond and post their own remarks. In Chapter 10, we show you how to capitalize on this.

If you're with a company that supplies products or services to pet-related organizations, you can offer product reviews, video demos or specific tips to help them manage their business.

Believe it or not, it IS possible to attract visitors to your business or practice via blogs. Fill your blog with interesting content, and all this new blog content is picked up by search engines to improve your organic search engine rankings. Some of your audience members may become regular blog fans and then become customers. It's that simple.

The Only Natural Pet Store blog is a fine example of how to create a visitor-attracting blog with customer-friendly posts.

The 5 top ways social media can help you grow your business:

- **Relationship building** — This is the best part of social media! You get to write about a topic you're passionate about, and at the same time, turn visitors into raving fans. When your prospects and customers are enjoying your posts, they'll follow what you're doing to the point of becoming big fans and loyal/repeat customers. Beyond that, many of these people are likely to become evangelists for your business and influence their friends and peers to do business with you, too.

- **Brand building** — Having a positive presence in social networks is a great way to raise brand awareness, boost recognition, enhance recall, and increase loyalty for your pet company or veterinary practice. For example, use your posts to reinforce your commitment to pet rescue and adoption, and the mission your business stands for.

- **Publicity** — When you have something exciting or important to share, it's easy to get the word out in social media. Share special events going on at your business, post cute pictures of pet customers, announce a new product line, announce a new video series and so on. You can also use positive posts to modify or address any negative perceptions.

- **Promotions** — Consider the coupon craze and the power of giving your fans exclusive discounts. People love deals, especially if you're giving them something that enhances their lives and supports their love of pets. In addition, exclusive "invitation-only" or "see-it-first" events can be very powerful with your social media followers. (Caution: If you decide to leap into Google+, note that Google+ does not allow contests on their business pages at this time. So far, companies are using Google+ to invite customers, fans and others to join their circle and, therefore, stay on top of what's going on there.)

- **Market research** — Think of social media as a great place to learn about your customers and find niche audiences. For example, you can use Twitter as a search engine of sorts. Simply type in a phrase such as "dog food" and see what people are talking about. Or, see what people are saying about your business! For instance…

- **Twitter:** Use www.twinitor.com, type in your company's name, town and state (if you rely on local customers) and any keywords you can think of that relate to your business… and voila! You'll see what people are saying.

- **Facebook:** Use Facebook's search feature www.facebook.com/srch.php to look for posts, photos, people, pages, groups and events related to your organization and your prospects' interests.

- **Google and Bing:** Sign up for Google Alerts (http://www.google.com/alerts), a free service that alerts you (by email or streaming news feed, your choice) when social media posts or website content includes topics that are relevant to your business. For example, if you sell veterinary software, sign up for "veterinary software" results in Google Alerts. You can also search for your product/service category in Bing News www.bing.com/news. For example, we typed "pet treats" into Bing News search and found articles about a certain brand recall that occurred just days before.

Follow the Social Media 80/20 Rule.

The first biggest mistake many marketers make in social media is talking solely about how wonderful they are or how great the company is. There's nothing more off-putting than a person who is self-absorbed, or worse, a pushy salesperson.

For instance, think about that person at a party who monopolizes the conversation about himself, doesn't ask any questions about you or how you're doing, and ends up trying to sell you life insurance.

Nobody wants to be "spammed" like this in social media. People look for entertainment value, such as fun pet images or videos, plus they like discussing news and events, discovering helpful pet care tips and connecting with others.

If you're a supplier — your prospects are looking for ways to increase profits while running a more productive business or practice. Show them ways to do that.

Therefore, be sure to balance your promotions with rich, magnetic content your fans really want to see.

* **Spend 80%** of your efforts interacting with others and being a helpful and fun source of information and entertainment.

* **Spend 20%** of your efforts promoting your products, services or special deals, etc.

Follow this rule no matter how much time you're spending, whether it's 1 hour a week or 5 hours a day. Check out other pet businesses of your type and see how they use social media. You'll learn a lot just by seeing the various posts and comments for each one.

Equally important: be part of the conversation. The second big mistake companies make with social media is that they slap it up and forget about it. (While researching pet-related blogs, we were amazed to see how many blogs had been created, yet no one has posted anything for over 6 months.) Take the time to comment on what your followers are saying, and thank them for commenting and for tagging your business in their photos.

7 Steps to Kick-Off a Successful Social Media Effort

NOTE: On average, it can take about 3 months for social media conversations to start flowing. Plan on posting about 4 times a week and engaging followers with questions about their favorite animals or topics.

1. **Set your objectives and goals.**

   Identify the primary purpose of your efforts. What are you trying to do?
   - Build awareness
   - Generate leads and sales
   - Improve loyalty and repeat sales

   Determine what would be considered a success:
   - More web traffic
   - Friends, fans, followers
   - Social mentions and goodwill

   Set S.M.A.R.T. goals (Specific, Measurable, Actionable, Realistic, Time-Based):
   For instance:
   - X number of fans in 12 months
   - Grow sales by 20% in 12 months
   - Increase appointments by 18% each month

2. **Determine the brand "impression" you want to communicate.**

   - Identify the key messages you want to project consistently across all platforms.

   - Always consider your USP: that Unique Solution Proposition or special something that sets you apart.

   - Write company profiles that focus on the prospect: why they'll want to engage with you.

- Be sure to clearly stand out: offer something delightful that differentiates you from everyone else.

- Always keep a short attention span in mind when you post messages.

3. **Find your best audience.**

Social media is a cluttered, crowded place. Identify where to put your focus — what tools will help you get in front of your ideal prospect on Facebook, Twitter, YouTube and/or your Blog.

- Identify your customer groups. (Revisit Chapter 2 if you're not sure.)

- Segment them into small sub-groups that might be congregating online. For example:
    - Pet parents looking for pet-friendly travel services.
    - Veterinary practice managers looking to increase cat wellness visits or senior pet wellness visits.
    - Dog agility clubs looking for versatile agility equipment.

- Research your marketplace to identify any sites or fan pages they're active within:
    - Facebook
    - Twitter
    - YouTube
    - Certain blogs, such as cat-lover blogs or horse-trainer association blogs

- Explore your current customer groups: What is their relationship with you?
    - Aware, but never purchased
    - Single purchase

- Repeat purchases
- Advocate of your brand

🐾 What does the audience know about you?
  - Nothing
  - Some awareness
  - Huge fan of your brand

IMPORTANT POINTER

Searching for your ideal customers in social media and monitoring the conversations for opportunities are super-important activities that can pay you back with more visitors and sales.

Therefore, devote some time to this. Block out an afternoon to get started. As we mentioned earlier, you can use www.twinitor to see what people are saying in Twitter, and www.facebook.com/srch.php for Facebook discoveries.

Here's what you can do with the various opportunities you find:

🐾 A mom mentions that her family of four (one of them is furry) is planning a trip to your town, and they ask their friends and followers for suggestions on where to stay, where to eat, what to do that's fun, etc., in places that accept pets. You could chime in with recommendations and offer them a $5 discount coupon toward a visit to your dog wash service in case the furry friend needs a bath during the trip.

🐾 Or, you receive a Google Alert email for posts including questions about how to choose the right organic puppy food. You can reach out and answer their questions and become the go-to resource for pet food advice, etc. The people you reached out to will appreciate your generosity and share that information. They'll buy their organic puppy food from your pet food store, of course!

4. **Hunt for fresh ideas to talk about in social media.**

Stay current on what's happening in your industry, and research what your ideal customers are looking for.

- Read what others are saying in your industry:
  - Websites, blogs and press releases
  - E-books and books
  - Industry periodicals (offline and online)
  - Twitter feeds by prominent people in your industry
  - Podcasts
  - Online videos from your industry

- Keep an eye on pet news and trends with these tools:
  - www.Google.com/alerts: As mentioned, sign up for Google Alerts by typing in relevant phrases such as dog, cat, horse, pet, etc., and receive streaming or batched email results from the web. Also, search Bing News for topics and trends related to your products and services.
  - Technorati: Subscribe to this leading blog search engine to stay informed of industry blog posts.
  - Trendrr: Visit this site to see how your brand or product is trending compared with others. Trendrr uses comparison graphing to show relationships and discover trends in real time.

5. **Create great content.** The right words matter… more than you know.

- Write in your own voice, making it personable (people follow people, not brands!).

- Use the same language and tone your target audience is comfortable with.

- Keep the content rolling (blog posts at least 1x/week, other social sites more often).

- Be open and honest.

- Meet your target audience's expectations: reply to comments, answer questions, reach out.

- Consider this every time: What benefits do they receive after reading your content?

  For example, write a post along these lines, "We're happy to announce that Sadie is recovering very nicely following her hip surgery with our new laser equipment. She was up and walking quicker than we expected, with no signs of discomfort! We'll post pictures later today after Sadie enjoys some private time."

- Be sure to include relevant keywords in your social media content whenever possible, including your page names, profiles and even status updates. For example, your blog post titles might be along the lines of, "How to trim cat claws the easy way," or "Myths and facts about dog massage." They all help with your search engine results.

Here are some fascinating facts we found for Facebook content best practices:

- **Posting 1-4 times a week produces 71% higher user engagement** than 5 or more posts for retail brands: quality trumps frequency.

- **Posts containing fewer than 80 characters produce 66% higher engagement** than longer posts (wow!).

- **Posts containing questions generate more than double the amount of comments,** even if they may get fewer "likes."

- **Top retail sales keywords that produced more user engagement:**

"$ off" and "coupon" worked best (55% higher user engagement rates); while the words "sale" and "percent off" (or % off) produced the lowest; even posts about offers less than $10 off produce 17% higher engagement than percent-off posts.

* **The 2 most effective types of posts contain a single photo attachment or use only words.** Posts containing only words produce 94% higher engagement than average. (Again, wow!)

* **Wednesday is the best day to post,** although you obviously shouldn't post ONLY on Wednesday.

Source: http://www.buddymedia.com/newsroom/2011/09/introducing-our-latest-research-a-statistical-review-for-the-retail-industry-strategies-for-effective-face book-wall-posts/

6. **Share, discuss and connect with your "peeps."**

As we mentioned in our 80/20 Rule… spend more time building relationships and communicating with your ideal peeps (your target prospects) than promoting your organization.

As you create and share more and more amazing content, your online audience will grow organically. The number of loyal followers will grow.

Here are some ways to make all of this WORTH IT.

* Post useful messages across all your social media platforms, such as your extended holiday hours (retailers) or "See you at SuperZoo (Booth 2111) or the North American Veterinary Conference (Booth 3665)!" (if you're a supplier).

* Drive people to your website for more info regarding a specific event, new product or service.

- Keep the relationship alive.

- Don't neglect your fans once the connection has been made.

- Keep them engaged by sparking conversations and sharing common interests.

Want proof that this works? Platinum Paws announced a new shipment of duck feet treats on their store's Facebook page, and sold out the treats that day. Wow.

7. **Schedule your social media.**

Now that you know what to post and who to post it to... the next step is to create an easy-to-follow schedule for your efforts.

If you don't schedule your efforts in a systematic way and then track them, how will you know where you want to end up, or how you're doing?

To put this into perspective, we like this *Alice in Wonderland* conversation when Alice is talking to the Cat:

"Would you tell me, please, which way I ought to go from here?"
"That depends a good deal on where you want to get to," said the Cat.
"I don't much care... " said Alice.
"Then it doesn't matter which way you go," said the Cat.
"... so long as I get SOMEWHERE," Alice added as an explanation.
"Oh, you're sure to do that," said the Cat, "if you only walk long enough."

The key to not wandering around like a lost pup in social media is to **schedule it:**

- Chart out and manage social media time on a calendar.

- Include your posting and monitoring frequency.
- Keep track of when people re-tweet your Twitter posts and "like" or comment on your Facebook posts.

Here are some examples to show you how to do this. We assume you already have a Twitter profile, Facebook Fan Page and blog setup. If you need help setting up your social profiles, the web resources in the back of this guide may be able to help you.

Example 1: 30-minute/day social media plan

15 min.: Content creation
Write a blog post about the latest new service you offer, and include a related tip that helps your audience.

5 min.: Content sharing
Post on a short summary on Facebook and Twitter linking back to your Blog.

5 min.: Connections
Search Facebook and Twitter for more people to connect with.

5 min.: Community building
Monitor your Facebook Fan Page community, respond to comments, and start a new conversation.
"Like" other Facebook pages.

Example 2: 30-minute/day social media plan

Plan to set this up in 60 minutes per month of content and video creation.
Devote 1 hour per month to write 16-20 posts at one time that you'll use throughout the month. This will give you more time for community building each day.

5 min.: Content sharing

Create a new written blog post or one with a video of your pet customers doing something cute related to your business (such as your store's pet Halloween costume contest). Also post it on YouTube.

10 min.: Connections

Search Facebook and Twitter for people you want to connect with.

15 min.: Community building

Join a Facebook Fan Page and have a conversation. "Like" other Facebook pages.

This will give you a great starting point to build upon. As you get comfortable with this process, check back with us at www.Pawzoola Publishing.com to find additional resources.

In Chapter 14, we show you how to measure the effectiveness of your social media efforts.

Two more important social networks for your pet business or veterinary practice.

You may be wondering why we didn't focus on LinkedIn yet. Well, it's a bit different from the big 4 that we talked about.

That's because LinkedIn is more of a "colleague network" — where your pet-industry peers and other professional connections can discuss the business side of marketing, and promote each other.

Someone recently explained the difference in this way (we're paraphrasing):

Facebook and Twitter are for socializing with consumers, buddies, family members, celebrities and brands.

LinkedIn is for business networking.

LinkedIn is a great tool for connecting to your pet-related community, including peers, vendors and marketers.

* With LinkedIn, you can connect with your professional peers and discuss similar challenges with them.

* You can join pet-business or veterinary marketing groups, such as
  * Pet Online Marketing Group (Dogs, Cats and More), and
  * VetDVM: Veterinary and Pet Businesses.

* The more you participate in group conversations in a helpful way — the more goodwill you spread for yourself!

Finally, you'll also find a lively and supportive group of professionals at PetIndustryTV.com, the Women in the Pet Industry Association and the Women's Horse Industry Association. These are great places where like-minded marketers come together to bounce marketing ideas off each other, find fresh strategies and gain support. Plus, receive valuable tips you can use immediately to find more customers and profits.

A note about Google+: Since Google includes its own products when providing search results, it's very important to establish a Google+ profile for yourself AND your business. Fill it out completely and start connecting with customers and colleagues. Google offers a great "Getting Started" page here: www.google.com/+/learnmore/getstarted/guide.html.

In Chapter 13, we show you how to include social media in your Profit Producing Planner.

But first, let's move on and discover some other powerful marketing methods.

CHAPTER 7 SUMMARY/ACTION ITEMS:
Connect with Fans Through Social Media (Online Networking)

* Once your website is optimized for traffic and sales, it's just as important to plan for how you'll connect with your prospects and turn them into buying customers.

* Social media is exploding as a way to reach your prospects, turn them into fans and then convert them into visitors and evangelists for your business.

* Be sure to follow the best practices of Facebook, Twitter, YouTube and Blogging to start engaging with prospects in a powerful way.

* A big part of social media success is finding the places where your target audience(s) are congregating; the groups and sites they flock to when discussing pet services, care, products and other topics related to the industry.

* You can get started right now by following our 7 Steps to Kick-Off Your Successful Social Media Efforts!

CHAPTER 7 Additional Notes:

chapter **8**

Generate More Opportunities with Email and Enewsletters

Bring in more business with emails your fans WANT to receive from you

Is email still an effective marketing tool? You bet!

Despite the surging growth of social media and other marketing methods, and despite the fact that consumers get an average of 362 emails a week[1]... email is still leading the way for many marketers.

Consider these findings:

* 91% of businesses use email marketing according to a recent study conducted by email service provider Constant Contact. Among them, 78% say such efforts are effective (32% "very" and 42% "moderately").[1]

* Email has brought in $40.56 for every dollar spent in 2011. This is higher than search efforts ($22.24), Internet display ads ($19.72) or Mobile Marketing ($10.51 and growing).[2]

* More than 50% of consumers make purchases as a direct out come of email in a survey conducted by ExactTarget. Email also drives more ROI (return on investment) than any other channel,

including social media and PPC (Pay-Per-Click) advertising.[3]

* 90% of consumers go online to send and receive emails every day as reported in DoubleClick's Annual Consumer Email Study.[1] This seems true enough when you think about your own email habits and those of your co-workers, friends, family members, etc., and especially when it includes checking email on smartphones.

    1. Source: www.marketingprofs.com

    2. Source: Direct Marketing Association 2011 study

    3. Source: http://blog.email-list.com/email-marketing-facts/email-marketing-in-2011-industry-facts-and-statistics/

Email marketing is still wildly popular because it's fairly inexpensive and people DO respond. As we mentioned before, 69% of people who subscribe to emails from a brand say they look forward to receiving their emails.

Once your prospects give you their email addresses and permission to contact them, you can regularly communicate news, information and special promotions they'll value… and this leads to repeat sales from a loyal following.

Plus, email marketing doesn't need to be difficult or time-consuming. There are a number of do-it-yourself online relationship-building services available that set up the entire format for you… and track your customer emails and responses. These helpful email marketing services include MailYourMarket.com, ConstantContact.com, MyEmma.com, Aweber.com and MailChimp.com.

Once you select one of their templates, you'll add your logo and make sure the design matches your brand identity so your readers will recognize it as an email from you. Then, you're ready to start sending messages.

You simply create each email message, hit send and presto! Your customers open an exciting new message from you and respond by buying more products and/or services.

So, which types of emails work best?

Let's start with the three main types of emails you should be including in your marketing, and then we'll share best practices to make sure your emails work their magic for you.

These are the three primary email types you can use to increase traffic and sales.

* **Autoresponders (Trigger Emails)**

   When prospects accept your email signup invitation online and give you their names and email addresses, they should receive a confirmation message along with a series of 5 to 7 welcome emails that "introduce them" to your business or practice and enlighten them on all you offer.

   This can be set up as an automated series (thus the term "autoresponders"), triggered by the initial email signup.

   These messages are not time-sensitive. Instead, they're designed to be "evergreen," giving you a way to help all new email list members begin a long and enjoyable relationship with your business, no matter when they sign up.

   To be truly powerful, each message should include a call-to-action that drives prospects to your website, learn more or make a purchase. Make sure your call-to-action links to a specific web page that's relevant to the topic in your email. For example, "Check out our unique, customized coupon center" should land on a specific page about this center. This will give you the highest response.

   Your autoresponder message sequence may look like this, staggered over a period of days or weeks:

- **Confirmation and Thank You**
  Thank the person for subscribing and explain that you'll be sending emails from time to time, to keep them informed on all the exciting benefits of doing business with you. Be sure to ask the prospect to "whitelist" your email address so your subsequent emails don't get caught in spam filters. Depending on which email service you use, this message may also include instructions to click on a link to confirm their subscription.

- **Welcome — Introduction to Our Business/Products/Solutions**
  You can assume that your new email list member may not know much about your business or what you offer that's special. He or she may have just discovered it and is excited about the idea of what you offer... but may not know exactly. Therefore, introduce some of the unique and delightful features of your solutions, including member-only discounts, free clinics or webinars, etc.

- **Enjoy Exclusive Benefits as an Email Subscriber**
  Reward your new list members for signing up. After all, they certainly didn't have to sign up. Give them a taste of why they made a wise choice to let you into their email in-box. Tell them about exclusive offers and discounts you'll email them from time to time. Explain that they may often be the first to know about new products, services or other features. Make them feel like an "insider" who is special, recognized and connected.

- **Did You Know... ?**
  Provide your new email list members with fascinating facts about your business, in ways that benefit them. For example, "Did you know we have a special Pet CPR training night at our clinic?" Or that "Thursday evening is Bring a Friend, Save 50% night?" Give them the scoop on desirable amenities and benefits they may not know about.

- **Join the Conversation**

  Invite your new subscribers to your social media communities and your blog. Explain what they'll find on your Facebook page, Twitter account, YouTube channel and Blog posts. Link to each one so they'll immediately join you there. This could even be separated into 4 individual emails.

These examples give you a starting point for powerful autoresponder emails. With your imagination and USP (Unique Selling or Solution Proposition), we're sure you'll think of other great topics to feature in your automated welcome series.

This is an example of a Welcome email that introduces new members to a valuable service:

Single-Topic, Time-Sensitive Emails

Email is a great way to announce something fresh and intriguing to your subscribers — whether it's a new service, a holiday party for members or a special discount or deal.

You already know that your subscribers love pets. And, you know they'll appreciate new and different ways to treat their pets, keep them healthy and happy and share the joy with others.

Therefore, consider your emails as "Public Service Announcements" that charm the heck out of your prospects. Bring them back to your store, practice or website again to see something new, buy gifts or take another action that brings in more profits for you.

Here are just some of the many topics you can promote in your single-focus emails if you're marketing to pet owners:

- Join us for a themed costume party, safety training event or other presentation this week
- Be the first to try our new service
- Meet our team
- Check out our new gift ideas for the pet lovers in your life
- You may be surprised to know... (facts/benefits about business)
- Holiday gift ideas
- Special discounts for a limited time
- Bring a friend or get a friend to subscribe (2-for-1 deal)
- Become a member of our club and get these benefits
- Join us for a ribbon-cutting ceremony
- Help us support rescue animals
- Meet local dog trainers — an invitation
- Have your pet's birthday party here (with special reasons why)
- Go on a fun hike with us
- Win an iPad (or other type of contest)
- Highlight a new product or service
- How-to pointers when using your product or service

Here are some topic ideas if your business is marketing to other pet companies or veterinary practices:

- Stop by our trade show booth to see what's new
- Be the first to try our new service
- Meet our new team at the upcoming conference
- You may be surprised to know... (facts/benefits about business)
- Special discounts for a limited time
- Become a member of our club and get these benefits
- Watch our latest demo video
- Check out our latest Case Study: how one business saved $XXX
- Learn how to [do something] faster, easier, cheaper at our free webinar
- Ask the experts: a teleconference featuring our distinguished panel
- Win an iPad (or other type of contest)
- Highlight a new product or service
- How-to pointers when using your product or service

 IMPORTANT POINTER

Focus on "What's in it for Me?"

The trick to getting a great response with each email is to always craft your email messages in a personal, what's in it for the reader way. And of course, include a call-to-action that drives a response — visit a specific page on your website, save now, etc.

The following veterinarian-focused email includes a strong reason to "read this now."

The following pet-parent-focused email hits on a topic that's important in the winter.

Now let's look at the third type of email you'll send, and then we'll provide a list of email message best practices you can apply to all three types to ensure great response rates.

❀ Enewsletters

Email newsletters, known as enewsletters, are still very popular when they include exciting news, "fascinating facts," special invitations and offers that appeal to the reader, and other enticing reasons to spend a moment reading about your business or practice.

Speaking of reading your news, we've heard that email recipients in general spend about 51 seconds reading the average newsletter.

This may not seem like much time, but when you consider that people only spend 3 to 6 seconds reading a Twitter tweet, a web page headline, or other marketing message... you can do a LOT with 51 seconds — as long as you make every second count.

The best enewsletters are packed with newsy, fun, beneficial information that's 100% focused on pleasing the reader and feeding their interests in dogs, cats and horses... or in business success (if you're a supplier).

To show you what we mean — here's a nice example of a local humane society newsletter with updates and a main article:

And, here's a veterinary-industry newsletter with topics listed at the top for quick scanning, and with details further down for those who are interested.

Now that you're familiar with the three main email types, let's look at general best practices that help you craft great emails every time.

5 Fundamental Guidelines to Crafting Great Emails

Make a HUGE difference in your email responses by following these 5 best practices.

1. **Segment and personalize your list if possible.**

   Remember in Chapter 3 when we talked about your different target audience groups?

   If you're marketing to pet owners, consider that new pet parents, senior pet owners, shelter volunteers and other pet fans will have different interests in your business and what it offers them. And, email is a fantastic way to reach out with information they WANT to receive.

You may have your own email list(s) that you grow through your website — offered with an incentive, such as a free shopping bag, pet-related ebooks, a free grooming or boarding visit pass or some other perk.

But also consider renting target-audience email lists from a broker, so you can reach audiences who may not have seen your site or heard of your business. To see how list brokers work, visit www.TheListWarehouse.com. *(Be sure to look in our Resources section for their special offer.)*

You can also ask your industry allies to share their list or promote you and send folks to your site. Once people come to your site, they can sign up for your own list.

When you have your lists ready to go, be sure to send messages that are perfect for each audience. A message to volunteers will be different from a message to first-time puppy owners, for example.

Ideally, you will personalize your messages by capturing the first name in your email signup box. It's been proven that a personal-looking message can lift response, so consider sending messages that begin with,

"Dear Margaret," or "Hello Bill!"

This personal approach is very easy when you use a professional email service provider. Simply set up your message with an automated "Personalize" field.

Finally, to make sure all recipients feel comfortable with your emails, clearly communicate your privacy policy so your recipients understand you won't be selling your list. They'll feel more secure about receiving your emails.

2. **Create inviting subject lines so your target audience will OPEN the email.**

When you check your email in-box and scan new messages, what's the first thing you notice? Quite often it's the subject line... and it prompts you to either open the message, instantly delete it, or possibly save it for later.

The same thing is true for your audiences.

If you want your readers to instantly open your messages, use those 48-50 subject line characters and spaces (before cutoff in most email preview panes) to your full advantage.

Make sure the subject line delivers a "why read this?" answer. Start with the "what they get" benefit and then follow with the what, how, why or other feature.

Here's an example: Get a Free Photo of Your Pet During Our July 4th Party!

A colleague of ours was involved in creating a recent Target Marketing email report in which hundreds of thousands of emails were analyzed. Here are some of the top email subject lines that are relevant to retail stores, pet service providers and others. Notice that they all focus first on what the reader gets... either a savings or a solution:

- The Perfect Gift is Just a Click Away
- HOWL-O-WEEN Savings, Treats & Events – Book Early!
- Up to 30% Off Your Order
- Be the First to See These Special Deals
- Final Day for Holiday Savings – Book Now

3. **Use the power of one.**

With the exception of enewsletters, which feature several newsy topics and links — your emails should always focus on one main idea and one call-to-action.

Here's why. The more ideas, links or features you add to your message, the more distracting it gets. And, those distractions cause the reader's mind to wander away from the action you want them to take. The result? Little or no action.

Be sure each email has one main desirable benefit or promise for your reader, with a relevant story or supporting points that back it up. Appeal to one core emotion: saving money, seeing something new, being the first to see it, being a pet's hero... anything like that.

In addition, give the reader one specific action to take in each email, whether it's shop now, make an appointment now or something else.

Plus, your link should take the reader to a web page that shares that single focus, such as...

- "Shop for holiday gifts now" leads to your web store page featuring pet gift ideas
- "Make an appointment now" leads to a web page featuring the specific event or service you're promoting, with clear signup instructions.
- "Be the first to try these riding gloves" leads to a page introducing a new line of riding gloves, with a special discount for trying them now.

4. **Design for all types of in-boxes.**

Never assume everyone is using the same email platform or seeing your email messages in the same way. Between Outlook, Apple Mail, Gmail and other systems, plus various computers and operating systems, your readers may be all over the place when it comes to "seeing" your email.

For example, if any of your readers have turned off the HTML graphics part of their email platform and your email message is mostly embedded in a graphic, it's invisible to those folks.

You can avoid this by creating two versions of your message: a fun-looking HTML version and a text-only version. Most email service providers allow you to do this very easily in seconds.

5. **Lead your readers to great landing pages.**

One of the biggest mistakes in email marketing is poor links. Or should we say poor landing pages. The following scenario happens way too often:

You've got eager pet fans who open your email message. They like what your email has to say, and they're ready to click on the link to buy something (food, toys, gifts etc.). But, when the click leads them to your home page or a busy page with lots of options, they're immediately confused or lost. Where's the topic from the email? What do I do now? The abandon rate is very high when this happens.

You want to avoid this common scenario and make sure you capitalize on that great opportunity your email worked so hard to create.

So instead, make sure your landing page is clear, relevant and focused — completely finishing the "buying sequence" you started in your email.

Here's landing page focused on ordering a free product sample:

There you have it. The best practices for email success.

Want something even easier?

If you're a pet or feed-and-farm retailer with a bricks-and-mortar store, you don't have to worry about all the suggestions we've outlined above.

You can simply sign up for PawsitivePerks.com/pet, an autopilot email marketing system that does all the work for you. All you do is sign up customers by asking them if they want to receive rewards for their purchases, and then swipe their card or ask for their phone number whenever they buy from you.

That's it! The rest is up to Pawsitive Perks, a system that sends out personalized, pet-parent friendly emails that tap your customers on the shoulder with a thank you for being a customer, and gives them customized, appealing rewards offers that bring them back to your store more often. For more details on how this works, visit www.PawsitivePerks.com/pet.

Finally, another important step is to measure the success of your email campaigns and really study which subject lines, messages, and links lead to the biggest clicks and sales.

More on Measurement in Chapter 14. But first, a look at the fascinating world of mobile marketing — coming up in Chapter 9.

CHAPTER 8 SUMMARY/ACTION ITEMS:
Generate More Opportunities with Email and Enewsletters

* For many marketers, email marketing is still one of the top ways to reach a target audience and bring in more visits and sales.

* Use the three main types of emails to frequently check in with your fans who signed up to hear from you:
  * Autoresponders
  * Single-focus emails
  * Enewsletters

* Set up a series of 5 to 7 welcoming emails after someone signs up to hear from you.

* Personalize your emails for the best results.

* Create subject lines that focus on benefits for the reader: Why should I open this?

* Make sure your single-focus emails do just that: focus on one intriguing main idea, reason to respond, and call-to-action.

* Be sure your email designs can be read in all types of in-boxes.

* Lead your readers to the appropriate landing pages.

* Measure your results and make tweaks to boost responses.

CHAPTER 8 Additional Notes:

chapter  9

Lure Local Traffic with Mobile Marketing

This section is mainly for businesses that rely on *local community customers:* pet supply stores, doggie daycares and boarding facilities, groomers, walkers, pet sitters, exercise facilities, veterinary practices and all others with a local emphasis.

Now you can steer smartphone users to your location through mobile tagging (including QR codes and tags), plus phone apps and mobile-friendly website versions.

Mobile Marketing is on the march, literally. Wherever people are, even in your neighborhood, they're using their smartphones as handheld search engines, social connectors, GPS devices and decision drivers.

Consider these mobile trends:

- Mobile searches have quadrupled in the last year. For many items or services, 1 in 7 searches are now conducted on mobile phones.[1]

- While SMS (texting) is the king of mobile messaging — with 8 trillion text messages sent in 2011 — consumers are also embracing mobile email and tagging in growing numbers.[1]

- Over 300,000 mobile apps have been developed in the past 3 years.[1]

- By 2015, it's predicted that 1 in 8 mobile subscribers will use m-ticketing and mobile sales tools in 2015 for airline, rail and bus travel, festivals, cinemas and sports events.[1] Right now, 1 in 4 Starbucks transactions are mobile, according to Starbucks. We're assuming this mobile-transaction trend will include community pet businesses and veterinary practices, too.

- On the average, Americans spend 2.7 hours per day socializing on their mobile devices. As a result, 3 billion tags have been printed on marketing materials in the past 6 months alone.[2] We'll explain tags in a moment.

  1. Source: http://mobithinking.com/mobile-marketing-tools/latest-mobile-stats
  2. Source: http://tag.microsoft.com/what-is-tag/home.aspx

Let's start with this common question: What is Mobile Marketing?

It refers to marketing on or with a mobile device, like a "smart" cell phone or an iPad or other tablet.

This includes distributing promotional and advertising messages to customers through wireless networks, sending people to websites via tags and codes they scan into their phones, or having a mobile-friendly websites appear when people search for something on their phones.

The Mobile Marketing Association defines it as, "a set of practices that enables organizations to communicate and engage with their audience in an interactive and relevant manner through any mobile device or network."

Going mobile with tags.

Tags may be the fastest way to get your message and information in front of your customers using smartphones and tablets. All they need is a built-in camera and the appropriate app (more about apps in a moment) — and this practice is growing.

Tagging uses two-dimensional barcodes to provide data displayed on a smartphone and tablet.

The prospect uses his or her smartphone's camera as the reader, pointing it at the code on a printed document such as a brochure or postcard, and then the phone scans the bar code, decodes it and displays the corresponding website, app, text message, phone number or vcard (virtual business card) to be downloaded.

There are several types of mobile tagging codes. In this guide, we focus on the two that will be most useful in the pet industry; the QR (Quick Response) Code and MS Tags (Microsoft Tag).

Here's the basic difference between the two:

- A QR Code has the web address coded into a bar code, so when you scan the code, you see the web page URL (domain or address) and can open the link in your phone. It's the most popular format and has the largest number of apps supporting it.

- The MS Tag doesn't have the web address embedded in the code. When you scan it, the host needs to look up what it's set to deliver. For example, it can be configured to do many different things over time, including display a website, app, text message, phone number or vcard to be downloaded. The downside is... it's a little more complicated and not as widely used as the QR Code.

QR Codes and Mobile Tagging.

From its humble roots in inventory tracking, the QR code has emerged as one of the most useful tools for connecting the real world and the digital world. This code allows marketers to engage customers wherever they are, using measurable, effective, and budget-friendly digital marketing strategies.

When you place your custom QR code graphic on a postcard, brochure, sign or other printed item... people can scan the code with a "reader" on their smartphones (such as the iPhone, Android or other phone that accommodates QR Codes), and immediately open up the specific web page the code is designed for.

The web page should offer something exciting and specific, such as a discount coupon for a new product or service.

Here's what a typical QR code looks like. This one happens to lead you to an invitation to attend a free webinar offering more tips on how to profit from QR codes, presented by C S Wurzberger.

Why use a QR code for your marketing?

Retailers and manufacturers are using mobile tagging to drive product sales across a variety of products such as cars, wine, coffee, clothing, packaged food, pet supplies and more... at the point of decision when prospects are more likely to be in the proximity of the business (thus, using their cell phone).

This location-based interactivity is an exciting new revenue stream for these marketers, and it can be for you, too. Here's why.

Let's say one of your target prospects is fairly new in town and isn't aware of your pet supply store, grooming facility, veterinary practice, etc. She stops at the town's Visitor's Center with her family, and she picks up your brochure. The brochure includes a QR Code that connects the prospect to a special "welcome to our town" web page offering her a 20% discount when she purchases something at your store or makes her first appointment at your facility. This may entice the prospect to visit you immediately, thus beginning a long and beautiful relationship.

See how it works?

Other ways to go beyond traditional marketing and benefit with mobile tagging:

* **Go beyond the sign.**
  Signage is the tried-and-true method for conveying information to visitors. But, signage is limited in size and media flexibility and cost-ly to update.

  With mobile tagging, you can supplement traditional signage with engaging, multimedia digital content people can access by scanning a QR code affixed to the sign. Possibilities include:
  * videos of pets doing something funny or enjoying what you offer, motivating the viewer to inquire about your products or services

- helpful information delivered by experts, helping the viewer see you as a valuable resource

This content can be updated online as needed — there's no need to modify the signage or even the QR code affixed to it.

* **Go beyond the promos.**
Promotions are great — who doesn't love getting a discount or free-bie? But, a coupon earned is even sweeter (especially for you) when it's earned by opting in for a mailing list or posting pictures on Facebook.

With mobile tagging, these actions are a scan and a click away. Encourage visitors to scan a code and visit a mobile page accessible only from inside your store or facility, or at specific times of day. Ask visitors to upload photos, sign digital guest books, participate in scavenger hunts and more. Not only can you reward them for their activity, you can make the activity rewarding in its own right.

* **Go beyond the usual print advertising.**
With mobile tagging, you can enhance your newspaper ads, maga-zine ads and other print materials with a QR code that invites prospects to scan for a special web page offering a valuable coupon, pet tip or other desired offer.

Mobile tagging best practices and 8 action steps.

Even though Mobile Marketing is a new option within your marketing mix, the industry offers several best practices that we strongly recom-mend, no matter when or how you adopt mobile tagging:

1. **Determine what you want to drive people to:** a special offer, more info about a specific service or product, etc.

2. **Create the QR code and Tag.** See the following Important Pointer! for QR Code development resources.

3. **Create the custom web page you want prospects to land on when they scan the code.** Some Mobile Marketing companies offer integrated solutions that merge the code with a custom page creation tool and tracking features. (See the following Important Pointer! for more details.)

4. **Make the web content relevant.** "QR" stands for "quick response." Make sure the content is immediately relevant to the location or object they're viewing — don't just send them to the home page of your website.

5. **Make the web content mobile**. It is absolutely no fun (and often no use) to use a mobile device to view a web page designed for a standard computer monitor. Make sure all your content is optimized for mobile. Otherwise your customers' first scan will likely be their last.

6. **Share the QR code and Tag.** Add it to your posters, advertisements, product packaging, rack cards, signs, etc.

7. **Make sure customers have a "reader" on their phone.** Since this is still a growing industry, it's important to guide people on how to use your codes, how they'll benefit by doing so, and how to download the reader. Giving them a bar code reader link to download will ensure they scan your code immediately.

8. **Track and monitor your results.** Select a mobile marketing company that gives you the ability to measure your ROI (return on investment). How many people have viewed your page? How many forwarded it on to someone else? How many people purchased your offer?

IMPORTANT POINTER

A variety of tools and service providers can help you read and generate your QR codes and related landing pages. To locate a free scanner, go to gettag.mobi on your smartphone's browser or visit Microsoft.com/tags. To find a free "QR Code Generator," go to (http://qrcode.kaywa.com/). You can find more free options with a simple search online.

If you're looking for a more robust tool that creates your Codes and Tags, organizes them, gives you fully customizable web pages and tracks your results, go to www.Immediatag.com and tell them we sent you. Plus, to view a demo on how to profit from QR Codes visit www.WildlyProfitableMarketing.com or scan the code shown below:

Mobile Apps (also known as mobile application software)

Up until a couple of years ago, when we thought of apps, we thought about computer software that helps a user perform specific tasks, such as desktop publishing, email software, Microsoft office, QuickBooks, etc.

But now there's a gigantic field called mobile apps. This is software developed for handheld devices such as smartphones and tablets.

There are two categories of apps: those that generate income and those built for branding, marketing and customer service.

A mobile app for your business can cover these categories through the following:

- Hours of operation
- Pricing
- Directions
- Featured products and services
- Pet photos or videos related to your business
- Become a member
- On-the-spot supply purchases

Here's an example of a mobile app for Ben's Bistro in Roseville, California. This app was developed for Ben's by PawsitivePerks.com/pet, so the store owner didn't have to do much at all to set it up.

You can either develop a custom app for your location, or work with a template and brand it to your location.

- Custom app development is more expensive than template-based apps, but a custom app can allow you to offer a truly unique experience for your prospects and customers. You'll find custom app designers online by searching for "mobile app developers," "custom mobile apps" and similar keywords. Or, visit www.Idextrus.com, a reputable developer who designed the MyPetED.com mobile apps.

The screen shot below is for the MyPetED iPhone app.

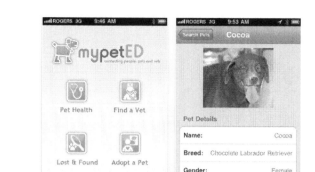

* Template apps are much more affordable and can offer you a wide range of functions and uses. In many cases, a template app will fit the bill just perfectly. To get more information about template mobile app options for pet retailers, visit www.PawsitivePerks.com/pet.

Mobile Optimized Websites

Only 33% of U.S. websites are optimized for mobile usage, according to the Mobile Marketing Association (MMA). Yet, as we mentioned before, 1 in 7 searches are now conducted on mobile phones for many products and services — and in many cases, mobile devices (phones and tablets) are increasingly replacing personal computers. This means you could be a pet industry pioneer by offering a great mobile experience!

The image that follows shows you the difference between a mobile-friendly version designed for the optimum user experience, and a regular website, viewed on a smartphone.

Mobile Website   **Standard Website**

So, how does your website look on a smartphone or mobile device?

Can folks easily find what they need when they're searching on their smartphones: your hours, products and/or services and directions? Or, are they forced to scroll around awkwardly, fumbling with navigation buttons that are too small... or not able to find what they need at all?

Ideally, you'll offer a mobile-friendly version as soon as possible. You'll certainly benefit from the effort!

When you do go for it and create a mobile version of your site, here are the best practices to follow:

- **Create a separate version with the most common information your mobile users seek.** This way you can provide easy-to-reach key info: directions, hours, products, services, events, etc. It improves the user-experience and satisfaction with your business.

- **Use text, not graphics, to display critical information such as your phone number.** The smartphone user looking for your phone number will want to simply click on it to call you, not type it in from a graphic you provide. Make sure your information is displayed for quick access to you.

- **Abbreviate the content.** You'll achieve better results when you adjust the content to quick, essential labels and statements (fewer words).

- **Minimize the design for a faster download.** As Apple's Steve Jobs said in 2010, ""The mobile era is about low power devices, touch interfaces and open web standards." So make sure your mobile-friendly graphics aren't overwhelming the mobile platform. Having said that, you'll want to be sure you don't compromise your branding in this version. It's recommended that you include your logo, colors and small thumbnail images as appropriate.

For the best marketing results with prospects and customers using their phones and tablets to interact with you, Mobile Marketing should be incorporated into your Profit Producing Planner and budget as soon as possible.

Your current web team may know how to create a mobile-friendly version of your site. If not, you can find reputable mobile site developers online, or you can get started with a click to www.idextrus.com.

CHAPTER 9 SUMMARY/ACTION ITEMS
Lure Local Traffic with Mobile Marketing

* Mobile Marketing is quickly emerging as a necessary addition to your marketing mix if you want to reach the growing number of people using mobile devices.

* Mobile tagging with QR codes is one of the fastest ways to dive in.

* Start with a clear purpose, add QR codes to select print materials that your prospects will see, and make sure you lead them to a web page designed to either complete a buying sequence... or extend a delightful experience.

* Mobile apps can also be powerful pet-fan tools.

* Consider offering a cool app to guide visitors through your organization or provide another helpful experience.

* Mobile-friendly website versions are also becoming important as more and more people view your website on their phones and other devices.

* You'll be a superhero by providing a clean, easy-to-read and easy-to-navigate mobile version with the key information most users expect.

CHAPTER 9 Additional Notes:

chapter 10

Bring More Web Surfers to You Through Online Advertising

Make an impact where your prospects are searching for pet-friendly products and services: use PPC, online ads and directories.

As we've mentioned in previous chapters, people are spending a lot of time online, searching for solutions. In fact, who uses the phone book anymore? Anyone? We're not sure.

All we know is, the web has taken over the phone book as the go-to place to find pet product suppliers, dog care providers, trainers, groomers, walkers, sitters, adoption shelters, etc.; the things you and other pet businesses offer. This is also true for industry suppliers.

We cover many types of online advertising or marketing approaches, but we'd like to start with the two most useful first:

* Pay-Per-Click (PPC) advertising
* Directory submissions

Here's the lowdown on each of these.

Pay-Per-Click Campaigns (PPC)

PPC campaigns are sponsored search engine listings in the form of mini-ads you pay for ONLY WHEN a prospect clicks on the ad to visit your website.

Our description below pertains to Google Pay-Per-Click (Google AdWords) because Google is the primary PPC service and we currently work only with them.

To show you what we mean, we typed this phrase into Google: "personalized pet gifts." Several relevant web pages appeared in the un-paid (organic) section of the search results, but also on the top and the right column, where paid ads appear. These are the paid results (sponsored ads) we saw:

These are PPC ads, and they may be appealing enough to drive people to the sites being promoted here.

So, how do you establish a PPC campaign? We've collected the best practices here, but Google also has great tutorials on creating effective PPC campaigns.

- **Start with the purpose of the campaign.**
  What's the message, who's the target and what do you want them to do?

- **Choose the right keywords based on your mission. (Revisit Chapter 6 for keyword tips.)**
  Make sure your PPC keywords and ad will match what your audience is looking for and also that it relates to the web page you're sending people to. If you're really feeling adventurous, you can create an Excel spreadsheet and create a list of different keywords to test.

- **Log into your Google account and set up a Google AdWords campaign.**

You'll find clear setup instructions when you set up your account. They have a complete library of user-friendly tutorials to help you find your way quickly and easily. (www.Google.com/AdWords)

* **Determine your ad price by bidding on certain keywords on a cost-per-click basis.**

   If the field for pet-care options in your community or pet gifts is crowded, and you want to show up above everyone else, you'll need to bid a higher amount for each click than if you have a very unique market niche with good/specific keywords.

   For instance, the bidding price is lower for something as specific or unique as **"Maine coon cat stuffed animals"** versus the more popular **"Siberian husky stuffed animals."** But – this is OK if you have the best selection of Maine coon cat stuffed animals… because the people who click on your ad will be delighted to find your selection. It would be harder to get all the traffic for "Siberian husky stuffed animals" since thousands of companies, including Amazon.com, offer Siberian-husky-themed items. Who knew?

* **Create your PPC ad message, following the simple rules of Google PPC ads:**
   * Your ad title can be up to 25 characters, including spaces.
   * Description line 1 can be up to 35 characters, including spaces.
   * Description line 2 can be up to 35 characters, including spaces.
   * Include the complete domain name of your website.
   * Tracking URL: a special landing page promoting the featured PPC product with a clear offer and call-to-action (this must be used so the customer immediately sees the information related to the PPC ad only).

Here's a screen shot of a PPC ad for "Siberian husky stuffed animals."

Siberian Husky Stuffed Animal
www.shopzilla.com/StuffedAnimals
Your Child's Favorite Playmate.
Find **Siberian Husky Stuffed Animal**!

HINT: Make sure you include a clear and appealing offer (a reason to get excited, such as "Save $50!") and a clear call-to-action ("Do this to learn more" or "Do this to buy at this discounted price").

If you bid the right amount per ad, PPC is a great way to enhance the visibility of your website and get new traffic.

Once you set up a PPC campaign, you're guaranteed to appear at the top of the page you choose a certain part of the time (as opposed to leaving yourself at the mercy of organic rankings, in which good positioning can be much tougher to achieve).

If your competition bids higher, they'll come up above you. So, you need to constantly monitor and tweak your bids.

It's super-easy to test different ad phrases and see which ones work better to generate response. In fact, PPC advertising can be a really inexpensive way to try various keywords for all your other online marketing efforts.

Also, you have full control of how much money you spend.

You can set your daily budget limit. For example, if your daily budget is $30, the ads will stop running automatically when you reach $30 worth of clicks, and then start again the next day.

You can also pause your campaign for a while by turning it off.

IMPORTANT POINTER

Avoid the mistake that **more than 80% of businesses make with their PPC campaigns!** They send prospects to their home page, and then the prospects can't find the specific promotion or product featured in the PPC ad. So, prospects get annoyed and leave the site.

Therefore, just like you do with your email links, make sure your PPC ad sends people to a landing page specifically created to feature your specific offer, product or solution — completing the buying sequence.

You can see why some industry gurus feel that PPC ads should lead your online sales efforts. The main reason is — you control the messages and you get to see, each day, how well they're doing to generate response.

Directory Submissions

An online directory is a catalog of web pages and information grouped by categories. This is a legitimate way of letting the World Wide Web know that your site and individual pages exist.

One of the most popular directories is DMOZ.org, in partnership with AOL search. This directory includes many categories you can select from to improve the chances of your site being found by your target audience.

DMOZ sponsors ODP, the Open Directory Project, with the mission of creating the largest, most comprehensive human-edited directory of the web. What's different about this directory is that it isn't automated like the others. Instead, it's maintained by a global community of volunteer editors who manually create the best results for a search. The ODP powers core directory services for some the most popular portals and search engines on the web, including Google, AOL, Lycos, DirectHit, HotBot and hundreds of others.

It's not difficult to submit your site to a directory. Here's how you can get started:

- Go to www.dmoz.org
- Look through all the categories and determine where your company best fits
- Click on "suggest a URL" located in the top grey bar
- Follow the step-by-step process

Niche-Focused Directories

Since there are over 1 trillion web pages on the Internet, it's getting harder and harder to get your site indexed on the first page of search engines. Therefore, more and more niche directory sites are sprouting up. They focus on one specific industry and compile lists of all the businesses in that industry.

For example: here is a pet-specific directory for pet parents.

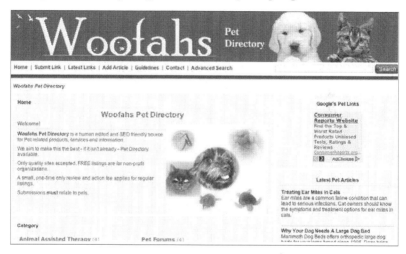

When done properly, niche-focused directories are a great way to drive more traffic and ensure your site gets indexed at the top for your search terms.

IMPORTANT POINTER

Before you submit your website to directories, make sure it measures up to the 43-point Usability Checklist in Chapter 4. You can only submit your site once, so make it great!

Just be aware that each directory has its own unique guidelines about where you can be listed and the kinds of links you can include. Once you take a look at some directories, you'll also see that they each have their own style. Your submissions can be tweaked for each directory.

Again, we aren't advocating that you manage directory submissions yourself. It can be time-consuming to become and remain directory literate, as this industry is constantly changing — just like everything else on the web!

Instead, the point of us telling you about directories is so you'll have a clue about what your web team recommends regarding directory marketing. You'll actually have fun seeing what they come up with for suggestions and evaluating the results!

Now we're ready to look at a few other juicy online marketing tactics you may want to consider.

Coupon/Daily Deal Sites

Although the daily deal trend seems to be leveling off, many Americans still make purchases via daily deal websites and related email promotions. Websites such as Groupon and Social Living lead the way in coupon/deal offerings, but many local and niche-industry sites also provide businesses with a new way to reach customers.

As a result of the coupon mania, pet-specific deal sites have sprung up in recent months, including dailydealsforpets.com, petching.com and mydailywoof.com. Pet parents are flocking to these websites for discounts on pet supplies, food, treats and more. Here's an example of what we mean:

Many businesses rave over these types of deal sites, noting that it's a great way to bring in new customers. Therefore, you may want to investigate the use of pet-focused deal sites for your business.

The world of daily deals and coupon sites is fairly new and the results for businesses have been mixed, so you'll want to be cautious when giving it a try. Here are some tips:

- **Be prepared for a quick influx of business.** Some companies offering a daily deal regretted the big rush of business because they weren't ready to fill so many orders at once. Be careful to offer deals you truly can honor in a short time.

- **Plan for follow up**. It's great to get dozens, hundreds or even thousands of new customers through a coupon promotion, but what happens after the new customers give you a try? After they make their initial purchase with you, follow up with compelling reasons to buy from you again or become a loyal customer. For example, make sure they sign up for your email newsletter so you can offer them product updates, special sale "sneak peeks," helpful tips and other appealing communications that drive repeat purchases and loyalty.

Banner Ads

You've seen them. Perhaps you've even clicked on them to go to a site.

Banner ads are those small, colorful, compelling ads that appear on most websites.

Here's an example of a banner ad, which can appear across the top of a website or on the side (usually on the right column).

You may wonder if these ads really work.

The answer is YES. That's why they're still around, even with Pop-Up Blocker.

In fact, good banner ads report a 1-3% click-through rate for each ad.

If your business is closely tied to the target audience for a particular site, it may be well worth your while to purchase a banner ad on that site.

Prices for banner ads will vary from site to site, and they're sold on a variety of websites and blogs.

If you're on a site viewed by your target audience and you want to show off your business to the site's viewers, look for the **Advertise With Us** button or link. Generally, this will take you to the advertising rates. And normally, it will give you pixel sizes for all the banner ads they're selling. You can either have your graphic person create the ad, or sometimes the seller will create the ad for you.

You'll know if your ad is working based on the number of click-throughs you receive to your site and by what happens when your prospects arrive at your location.

Of course, your ad must be very eye-catching, concise and compelling to motivate prospects to respond. And, be sure to link it to a focused landing page that finishes the buying sequence, as we've discussed before.

Ads on Industry Niche Sites with Phonebook-Like Directories.

This is quite similar to banner advertising, but your ad placements are on specialized websites that have directory listings for a particular business niche.

For example, we mentioned Woofahs-Pet-Directory.com before. This directory is specifically for dog lovers and dog businesses. You may want to advertise on this directory to promote your business.

Pet Blogs

In Chapter 7, we explained that blogs are incredibly worthwhile for attracting fans and customers to your website. We covered the how-to over writing your blog in depth.

Now, it's time to look at OTHER blogs that may send more traffic your way.

Imagine that a pet care authority, who is relevant to your business, posts blogs on her site to discuss topics your target prospects are eager to read.

If they are indeed eager, then this blogger has done a good job of reaching them and has perhaps even built a strong community of followers. You can often tell by checking the comments section.

So, this is your opportunity to join in. You could post a comment on this authority's blog and include a link to your site. The readers — your target prospects — might read your comment and click-through to your site. Voila! You've captured them.

To make this strategy super-effective for you, here are some "good blogger" guidelines to follow.

- First, your comment should be all about the blogger's topic and your reaction to it. It can NOT be about your business! That's a big no-no.

- So, if the blogger says something like, "Only a few U.S. pet retailers offer a truly green experience where all products and business practices are sustainable… ", you could say something like, "As a pet supply store that follows green practices, we know it's tough to maintain the lowest carbon footprint possible. But, we found that most of our customers are more than happy to embrace our products and efforts to minimize waste." Perhaps give a brief example. Then say, "If you want to know about this, feel free to contact me at [your email address, followed by your website's domain name]."

- See how we purposely steered away from bragging about how clever you are or why all the readers should flock to your site? A blogging comment needs to be neutral as far as promoting your business is concerned. Just make it a natural part of the blogger's discussion.

If you have important info to share, you could also ask about becoming a guest blogger with them. For example, PetCopywriter.com recently did a guest blog series on Pet-Sitter-Marketing.com.

To learn more about blogging, visit www.WordPress.com for free demonstrations, tips and "get-started" programs. Or, visit www.PetCopywriter .com/blog and www.PetIndustryTV.com for pet industry-specific tips.

Podcasts

Podcasts are popular marketing vehicles for creating all kinds of new sales opportunities.

Simply put, a podcast is a recorded presentation that people download from the web and play on their iPod, their mp3 audio player or their computer. Or, they just listen to podcasts on the website.

These presentations can be in the form of shows similar to "how-to" programs on TV or the radio, or they can be purely entertaining. You can find podcasts about the plight of rescue dogs, eco-friendly products and services for pets, off-leash dog park discussions, how to plan a party for pets, how to take care of puppies or kittens, or other pet-related topics. The possibilities are practically limitless for a pet-related organization.

Thousands of companies offer free podcasts on their websites as a way of attracting new customers or giving existing customers a reason to return to the site each week.

Podcasts may be a great vehicle for you, too. You could establish yourself as an expert on your pet topic, or you could host a program and interview other pet experts.

There are all kinds of possibilities. Of course, you'll need to make sure your podcast ultimately drives traffic that will become profitable for you.

Be sure to include the podcast transcripts on your site, too, so people can also read or print the text if they prefer. Plus, the text is great material for search engines to find on your site.

Linking Campaigns

Building a linking campaign is a very important part of your online advertising. Many search engines use link data in their ranking algorithms.

That simply means that when someone links to a page on your website, they're casting a vote to say this page is important or valuable, and you (a human or search engine) should check it out!

As you probably know, a link is a button, phrase, graphic or ad that's programmed to jump to another website when clicked.

In a linking campaign, the link is text only, using keywords, and looks like this:

Find personalized pet gifts featuring most dog breeds and many cat breeds.

When you click on this link phrase, you're sent to a relevant site, possibly called www.yourstorename.com/personalizedpetgifts.

You can use a linking campaign to get traffic from someone else's site to your site. And quite often, in return, your site would provide a link to the other person's site. This is called reciprocal links: "I help you and you help me."

This is a great way to build business relationships that are mutually profitable, plus search engines like reciprocal links, so it may improve your rankings.

When you do it yourself, link campaigns are usually free and can be quite useful if you're set up as a link on a site that's relevant and very popular with your target prospects.

The trick to successful linking campaigns is to choose popular, quality websites your target prospects are likely to visit.

Your web team will use the following quality indicators to evaluate sites you're considering for a linking campaign.

* **Domain age** — How long has the site been around?

* **Incoming links from .edu and .gov** — These rank higher than .com for credibility.

* **Quality directory listings** — For example: DMOZ.org, Dogster.com and other niche industry directories.

* **Deep link ratio** — How many levels of links are involved, how many are relevant, and how many pages are involved?

* **Page rank and link popularity** — How does the site rank in search engines? Google Toolbar is a quick easy way to check this.

* **Number of pages indexed** — How well is the site indexed and recognized by the search engines?

CAUTION: Don't sign up for automated link-building software — The search engines don't like these.

To build an effective linking campaign, your 3 options are to:

* Do it yourself: Assign someone on your own staff to approach different website owners directly and request links to your site,
* Ask your professional (outside) web team to manage it, or
* Hire a link-building company yourself and have them do an effective, reliable job for you. Be sure to ask for references if you consider hiring a link-building firm such as www.LinkVehicle.com.

Want to try and do it yourself? Here's an overview.

1. Identify which website pages and keywords you want to show up in the search engines.

2. Create a list of companies you'd like to be connected to.

3. Sign up and submit your site to niche directories.

4. Check who's already linking to your site and your competitors' sites. For example, if we want to see who is linking to a particular business such as Doctors Foster & Smith, we go to a search engine and type in link:www.drsfostersmith.com and click enter, as shown in this graphic. We then get a list of all the web pages that are linked to them.

Two Little Fishies - Links
www.twolittlefishies.com/tlf_links.html?lang_id=5
Esta lista de Links é continuamente atualizada e inclui nossos revendedores e sites onde você pode encontrar informações úteis sobre aquários, recifes de ...

2011 Sweet 16 Picnic - Pups Without Partners Greyhound Adoption
www.pupswithoutpartners.org/picnic2011.htm
2011 Sweet 16 Picnic. Picnic Pup Sunday June 12th, 2011 11:00 AM - 4:00 PM Rain or Shine. Osbornedale State Park (directions) Chatfield Street Derby ...

Pets at Home UK - www.petsathome.com petsathome
www.joeant.com/DIR/info/get/5230/148671
Buy pet supplies online or find a local store. Products for dogs, cats, small animals, birds, reptiles, chickens, horses, fish and wildlife.

Garbage Intoxication/Food Poisoning in Dogs and Cats
www.peteducation.com/article.cfm?c=2+1677+1684&aid=2407
Sources, signs, immediate care, and veterinarian care of an exposure to a toxin known as Garbage Intoxication or Food Poisoning.

The Use of Melarsomine (Immiticide) in Dogs
www.peteducation.com/article.cfm?c=0+1465&aid=1438
Indications for use, side effects, dose, contraindications, drug or food interactions, toxicity, and signs of an overdose of Melarsomine (Immiticide).

Honey Dwarf Gourami (Colisa chuna)
www.peteducation.com/article.cfm?c=16+1911+1957&aid ...
The Honey Dwarf Gourami is sometimes known as the Honey, Sunburst, or Dwarf Gourami. Both the male and female are pale yellow-brown in color, except ...

5. Now, compile a list of sites you want links on and sites you want to link back to (remember reciprocal links help with search engine rankings).

6. Collect their contact information and begin emailing and calling them with a personal request or invitation. Keep in mind that businesses get "spammed" all the time with bogus link requests, so be sure to reach out as one business professional to another, with a reference or a reminder that you met the person at a conference, etc. And of course, include a "what's in it for me, the website owner?" reason to connect with you.

That's it!

CHAPTER 10 SUMMARY/ACTION ITEMS:
Bring More Web Surfers to You through Online Advertising

* Online advertising can offer very effective ways of attracting pet fans and potential customers on the web.

* The two most useful online advertising methods are:
  * PPC ads
  * Directory listings

* With PPC ads, you can increase website traffic by bidding on focused keywords and creating strong offers.

* Give PPC a try. It's easy to set up a campaign, and you control the schedule and budget.

* Submit your website to appropriate directories, so your site is included in the resources pet fans are checking out.

* Banner ads can give you great exposure and traffic from other web sites that attract your audience.

* Blogs and podcasts are also useful platforms for attracting more visitors.

* Link-building can also be powerful, especially if high-quality sites send prospects to your site.

CHAPTER 10 Additional Notes:

chapter  11

Make a Splash with Media and Sponsors via Public Relations (PR)

With today's mix of online and offline PR distribution services, niche-industry media, potential sponsors and reporters looking for fresh, interesting pet stories… you can rake in great publicity for your organization by making the most of your news releases and event announcements as well as local community outreach and sponsorships (if you're a nonprofit).

So, let's take a look at the fun world of PR and sponsorships.

"50% of the public now cites the internet as a main source for national and international news."

— Pew's Research Center 2013

Imagine reaching larger audiences for very little money.

News releases about your organization's features can be a great way to share your messages and draw more visibility to your location. Plus, when they're optimized properly with keywords (see Chapter 6), your announcements will be indexed and found in the search engine results.

PR has the power to reach millions of fans and distribute your stories to mass media such as newspapers, magazines, television, radio and various online blogs and venues — all at a low cost to you.

Your only cost is the time to develop the news releases, mail them, and distribute them online through services that charge a fee (but are worth it).

Therefore, your PR efforts should focus on promoting goodwill between your organization and the various target audiences within your local community, the media and fans across the web.

Your announcements can include new services, special events, stories about your pet customers, new trends, wonderful rescue stories, quirky pet stories and other information for pet fans everywhere. If you are a pet-industry supplier, you can announce a roll-out of new products or services, case studies, problem/solution, etc.

When you create newsworthy releases and get them to the right outlets, you can expect these specific payoffs for your business:

* Thousands of people discover specific offerings only you can offer in your unique way.

* You continue building a great image for your business.

* You'll keep your business front and center in your prospects' minds when they're searching for great solutions, either in your community or online.

* You can out-promote your competitors.

* You'll enhance your credibility as a high-quality resource.

* You'll see your traffic and business grow and grow.

* You'll enhance existing relationships with prospects, customers, sponsors, the local community and the pet professionals community.

* Attract attention to a new product or services you are offering.

* You'll penetrate new markets and attract new potential visitors.

What's not to love about PR?

Now, let's find out how you can approach PR in the smartest way.

IMPORTANT POINTER

Your news releases will have different names depending on where you're sending them.

* A press release is for print media and online distribution.
* A media release is for radio and TV.

The following release is a great example of what you'll send to the various media outlets that are perfect for your pet-related business:

For immediate release

Independent Pet Retailer Reports Steady 12-Month Growth in Loyal Customer "Addicts" and Spenders

A new rewards card program is helping local pet supply stores attract more traffic and sales, even on historically sluggish days, with an affordable system that lets them compete with big box stores.

LAS VEGAS, NV February 9, 2011 – In mid-January, a major Nor'easter snowstorm had brought store traffic to a halt for the Blue Seal Feeds & Needs farm and pet supply location in Derry, New Hampshire. But, in the middle of the day, a lady came into the store, dusting the snow off her coat and looking like she was on a mission. The manager said, "I can't believe you ventured out in this weather!" She said, "It's Double Points Wednesday!"

This is just one example of how customers have become addicted to the Blue Seal Loyalty Rewards Card, which offers valued reward points for every purchase in their store.

The Blue Seal rewards card system was developed by PawsitivePerks.com, the pet industry's first Customer Loyalty Rewards Card program designed to drive extra store visits and purchases for independent retailers like Blue Seal Feeds by rewarding customers with points and exclusive, customized benefits every time they shop.

Jerry Salvucci, Manager of Company Stores for the Kent Nutrition Group, Inc. (Maker of Blue Seal Feeds) said, "The Pawsitive Perks system has become a great way for us to offer something special to our customers that the competition doesn't have; in addition to providing excellent products and personal service. In just under a year, our 11 Blue Seal company stores have signed up more than 11,000 rewards members."

How has this growth in card membership affected sales for local Blue Seal stores? Jerry reported:
- "Members are using the cards at every visit, and are coming in more often to earn points.
- Recent numbers show that around 25% of our sales involve the loyalty card.
- In December 2010, 14,000 of our store transactions used the card.
- Thanks to Double Points Day, sluggish Wednesdays have become one of our busier days!
- New pet food customers are coming in and getting hooked with the card. They return once a month or every other week to buy food, and while they're here, they look in the pet aisle for other items we have."

Jerry summarized, "We're seeing an increase in overall transactions, and we believe there'd be a massive revolt if we tried to take this card away from our members."

Pawsitive Perks.com owner Kamron Karington added, "We understand how hard it is for independent pet business owners to continually compete with bigger stores while juggling the functions of their pet stores. We created Pawsitive Perks as an easy, affordable way to maintain customer loyalty and increase sales with a simple 'autopilot marketing system.' Store customers seem to be hooked, as Jerry mentioned."

Independent pet business owners looking for similar results can visit www.PawsitivePerks.com, where they'll find a tour of the Customer Loyalty Program and a link to request a personal consultation for their store. They can also call 800-724-7000, ext. 270, to speak with program advisor Kevin Kelly.

Contact
Kamron Karington
Repeat Returns / Pawsitive Perks
702-966-3001
Kamron@karingtongroup.com

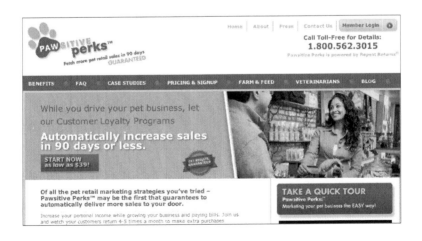

We'd like to thank PawsitivePerks.com/pet for allowing us to include this awesome sample in our book.

Next up, a discussion of how to distribute your releases.

Today, PR consists of three avenues: offline news releases, online news releases and a press page on your website.

* **Offline News Releases**

   Offline outlets will include print newspapers within your local radius, travel magazines, trade publications, local radio and TV stations.

   You'll distribute your stories by mailing, emailing and faxing them directly to individual editors and reporters at specific locations.

* **Online News Releases**

   You can easily release your news to the world and often get valuable coverage via PR distribution sites such as OnlinePRMedia.com, PR.com, PRWeb.com, PRNewswire.com and others you'll quickly find with a search for "pr distribution services."

   You can also subscribe to HARO.com (Help a Reporter Out) emails and watch for any reporter inquiries related to pet stories or pet-industry stories they're developing. You may find the perfect opportunity to be a primary source for a great pet or business magazine story!

   Both of these online news release strategies can offer you a very effective way to get the word out about your company or practice. Just be sure your news releases are written as strictly factual news items, not overly sales-y or promotional pitches.

Plus, you'll always want your news releases to include a link back to the most relevant page of your website.

For example, if your release is announcing a unique new mobile dog washing service in a particular community, link the news release back to your specific web page that features information about that dog wash service. Don't make the common mistake of linking back to your home page or other general page, because it will confuse the reporter or prospective visitor.

❧ News Releases in Your Website's Press Room

Here's a fabulous way to increase search engine traffic to your website: post your news releases on your site's own Press Room.

Be sure to make full use of a PRESS page on your site by adding fresh news releases whenever you have something exciting to announce, such as:

- New products or services
- Special events
- Awards or recognition
- Staffing changes (promotions, new hires, etc.)
- New technologies that help your audience
- Stories about the pets you serve: a clever dog who won a recent agility competition, a special cat rescue story, etc.

In the next screen shot, notice what a great job PetFinder.com is doing with their press page. It includes the latest releases, media contact information, a search feature and more.

When you post your releases to your website, use keywords in the headlines, links, photo caption, and other key areas within the release (but don't overdo it!). Just a few places will be fine. And, limit the links to your website to just two or three within the release.

All of this content will be picked up by search engines AND the media, giving your business expanded exposure.

Build your personal list of PR outlets and reporters.

We recommend compiling a list of all PR outlets you want to share news with on a regular basis. This makes it easy to practically "set it and forget it" each time you have a new story to send out. You could even develop a separate email list of PR folks in your automated email system. It's great to separate your overall email list into sub-groups like this.

Collect the following information for each publication, TV and radio station and website you wish to reach:

* Editor's or reporter's name

- Company/organization name
- Mailing address
- Email address
- Phone number
- Fax number

Plus, when building your media list, make a note on each outlet to identify:

- Where does the PR source distribute its news to?
- Who are their ideal readers? Do they align with your target audiences?
- What areas of special interest do they write about?
- How do they prefer news release submissions: via fax, email, an online form?

The more you know about them, including their deadlines, production schedules and audiences, the higher your chances for getting the story printed. It needs to be a win/win relationship for both of you. In other words, your news needs to be useful to them.

Over time, make an effort to build relationships with your PR partners. It's the key to successful PR campaigns.

With proper planning, you can build long-term, productive partnerships and momentum.

Now that we've identified both your offline and online media partners, let's look at how to put together your PR campaign.

5 Steps to Building Your PR Campaign for the New Media World

1. **Identify the story you want to share with the public.**
   What makes it unique, compelling news?

2. **Set your objectives for the PR release:**
   - Increase visits on "slow Wednesdays" by 28% through a special event announcement.
   - Announce an important new service at your business, with an example of how it has helped a local customer.
   - Educate the public about ways they can join in and help rescue abandoned dogs and cats.

3. **Prepare your draft message.**
   - Focus: What's the primary message you want reporters and your audience to hear, understand and remember?
   - Gather your facts, photos and videos if possible.
   - Ensure that your news is interesting and compelling.

4. **Write your release. (See our example in this chapter)**
   - Headline and story hook
   - Lead paragraph
   - The story
   - Quote from someone at your business, such as the owner, operations manager or trainer, as well a customer or client who benefited
   - Background info
   - Closing paragraph with info about the organization issuing the release.

5. **Submit your release and follow up with a phone call or email.**
   Make sure they received your story (ideally within 5 days of submitting).

Create a Fabulous Media Kit.

Your media kit is an informative packet about your organization. It's a great way for communicating key facts in a quick, efficient manner.

Your media kit should include:

* The history of your organization, including the date it was founded, why it was founded, how it has grown, etc.

* Basic fact sheet: the key products, services and solutions you offer, especially unique products or services in that community or the industry, etc.

* Bios on key leaders at your organization, with their photos and stories.

* Current press releases, media releases, copies of press clippings, video samples, relevant pet photos, customer testimonials, current calendar of events, etc.

This packet should be branded to match your organization's identity materials and website.

You don't need to go wild; 3 to 7 pages are fine. When putting it together, ask yourself, "Would I read this entire document?" or "Does this piece matter to a reporter?" If the answer is no, take it out.

Plus, we recommend making your media kit available for mailing or downloading as a PDF document on your website.

Finally, you may want to check out a more detailed source of public relations strategies. One of our favorite business authors, David Meerman Scott, recently wrote this guide: *Newsjacking: How to Inject your Ideas into a Breaking News Story and Generate Tons of Media Coverage.*

And now, a special section for nonprofits!

Sponsorship Opportunities for Your Rescue Shelter, Service Pet Training Program or other Pet-related Nonprofit Organization

We know that sponsorships (by individuals or corporations) are a big deal these days when it comes to getting a nice chunk of money for your organization.

Sponsors are looking for ways to build goodwill in the community and support worthy causes. That's where your pet-related location can help them.

Everybody wins when you connect with sponsors who are looking to reach the same people you're trying to reach.

- The sponsors get great publicity when you thank them publicly and include them in your materials.

- Plus, the sponsors can help you secure the much-need funding to support your efforts. Along with funding, they can provide you with products, pro-bono services and fundraising support. For example, they may:
  - Feature your organization on their website
  - Help you with promotions: emailing their database, sending out a direct mail piece
  - Arrange media appearances for you
  - Sponsor a contest with you
  - Team up to champion a cause
  - Launch a video series

How do you get sponsors?

First, include a Sponsorships web page on your site, with content on the reasons companies will benefit as your sponsors. This may include some of the same information as the PRESS page, but also include specific "Why Sponsor Us?" benefits and calls-to-action that invite potential sponsors to get in touch with you.

Next, follow these steps for reaching out to potential sponsors in your community through direct mail, networking and phone calls.

1. Identify a project or program that needs funding.

2. Create a list of ideal sponsors that align with your project. Learn everything you can about them: go to their websites and any industry-specific resources. Record your notes for reference.

3. Call to schedule a preliminary phone pitch to discuss your idea/request.

4. Develop the proposal: determine how much money you need, what resources they can provide and what benefits you can give them.

5. Write a cover letter requesting a possible sponsorship and include why it will be beneficial to their company. Also list out the specifics of what they'll receive for publicity and exposure if they come on board as a sponsor.

6. Mail them the cover letter along with a copy of your fabulous media kit. If possible, hand-deliver the packet for an added positive impression.

7. Follow up with a phone call within 5 days.

Another tip: Be active in your business community venues, such as Kiwanis Club meetings and Chamber events. You'll find ample opportunities to network with potential sponsors.

CHAPTER 11 SUMMARY/ACTION ITEMS:
Make a Splash with Media and Sponsors via Public Relations (PR)

- PR doesn't have to be time-consuming or expensive to manage, but the payoffs can be priceless.

- Use news releases to get the word out whenever you have something that pet fans, your community and general pet-media or pet/veterinary industry reporters will find valuable, unique and news-worthy.

- There are three powerful avenues for your news releases: offline distribution (local newspapers, radio and TV plus national magazines), online distribution for websites and blogs, and your own website's Press Room for search engine optimization.

- Make sure your news release is written in a factual, newsy way — not as an advertisement.

- Include keywords in your headlines, links and other areas so search engines will pick up the content and rank the release in your Press Room.

- Create a Media Kit you can send to your outlets, to provide great background on your organization.

- If your organization is a nonprofit, sponsorships can be an excellent way to generate income for your programs.

- Follow our 7 steps to getting sponsors for your organization.

CHAPTER 11 Additional Notes:

Turn Offline Marketing into a Flurry of Traffic, Too

Offline marketing is your more traditional marketing — the type that's been around since way before the Internet came along. And, it's still extremely powerful as part of your marketing mix.

This category includes print materials such as rack cards and brochures; direct mail; voice mail messages; radio and TV commercials; signs; sell sheets; trade show materials; Chamber of Commerce materials and other traditional marketing pieces.

These materials and approaches can be very important to your pet business, veterinary practice or pet-industry supply business, and should be included in the marketing mix to drive traffic to your website, business and physical location.

These marketing approaches have been around for ages, yet we know it's always good to have a reminder of how best to use them for your organization and incorporate them professionally into your marketing mix for the best results.

The purpose of this guide is to show you how to integrate them as part of a multi-media action guide.

Rule #1 for your offline materials:

Make sure they all match your brand and your unique promise messages: the unique reason to choose you.

Everything your organization puts in front of the market — including all offline and online materials — represents your face to the world!

These materials should look like they came from the same place, with the same delightful voice that's unique to you.

Be sure to carry your organization's logo, colors, fonts, and other personality traits through every piece you create… reinforcing your brand awareness in the minds of prospects, customers, the media and other important audiences.

Now, what can you do offline to promote your business and bring in more customers and profits?

First, be sure to include or mention your location's website domain name on these offline materials.

* **Business identity materials:** These are your standard "collateral" materials for conducting business. They usually include your organization's name, contact information, website domain name, and perhaps your slogan or tagline:

  - Business cards
  - Letterhead sheets (also called stationery)
  - Envelopes
  - Signs
  - Answering machine and "on hold" messages
  - Invoices, statements and contracts

* **Traditional advertising/promotion materials:** These are the classic business materials that have worked well for all types of pet-industry companies (when done properly) including:

- Brochures and flyers
- Sell sheets
- Trade show banners and other materials
- Newspaper and magazine ads
- Direct mail postcards and multi-piece mailings
- Radio and TV commercials
- Coupons
- Presentations and handouts
- Printed media kits and press releases
- Billboards
- Sponsorship materials

IMPORTANT POINTER

Your offline promotion materials are great for reaching several audiences.

The following primary audience types are looking for what you have to offer. We can assume you're already doing some of the marketing approaches mentioned here, but you may find a few new ideas to support your efforts.

Local Pet Parents:
If you're a local pet supply or service business, or a veterinary practice, you rely on generating traffic and profits from people in your community.

Local advertising, including newspaper ads plus radio and TV commercials can be an excellent way to reach them — promoting the reasons why your business is a great choice for pet care and supplies. Use this advertising to mention special deals at your location and on your website, or invite them to check out your new mobile app.

Other Local Pet Businesses:
Local pet professionals can use offline marketing to refer each other for the benefit of all.

Reach out to them with brochures, flyers, letters and other materials they can post in their lobbies. For example, a local dog trainer could provide a set of brochures to a local veterinary practice, and vice versa. Local pet retailers can create discount coupons to hand out at the local doggie daycares.

Everyone wins when the community professionals support each other! Make sure your pet-industry community knows about your amenities and special features.

A note about Direct Mail:

Even though online marketing has exploded in the last few years, direct mail is still very powerful when you run a well-planned mailing with a super-appealing offer targeted to your audience.

When you have something to promote locally or to a targeted list even nationally:

- Set your goal, what you want the direct mail campaign to accomplish (Example: welcome new pet-parent residents to town with a money-saving coupon for your store)
- Determine exactly who you're going to target; new residents
- Define the demographic area (3 counties, all within an hour of driving to your location)
- Use your own list (if you have one) plus buy or rent an additional list
- Determine the type of direct mail piece you'll create:
  - Postcard (regular or oversized)
  - Newspaper flyer
  - Mailed letter
  - Type of material: green, recycled
- Plan your big offer (promise), detail content and call-to-action (visit this web page, call us, bring in this coupon)
- Track responses: use a tracking code or have customers bring the card in to redeem

* Follow up (a large percent of direct mail campaigns fail because there's no follow up)

For example, a simple letter to hotel owners, followed up by a phone call, has generated a dog-products company a tremendous response. The owner recently told us,

"I'm afraid to go to too many hotels at once because we need to be able to handle the first rush first. I don't want to get more large orders than we can handle at once and get a name for not producing on time."

Wow, imagine being concerned with becoming TOO successful. This just shows how direct mail can still be extremely powerful.

This highly successful direct mail example is a customized reminder postcard for a veterinary practice (we're showing the front and back).

Next, consider using these 7 additional ways to broadcast your organization and website through offline marketing:

- Put your domain name/tagline on your vehicles.

- Wear a T-shirt and/or ball cap with your domain name/tagline.

- Sponsor a local sports team and have them post a big sign in the park with a big enticing headline and your domain name/tagline.

- Sponsor networking events and make brochures available with your domain name/tagline.

- Hand out stuffed animals, labeled with your domain name/tagline, at local pet fundraiser walks and other pet parent-friendly events (with permission).

- Send your current customers or members a postcard with a discount coupon for purchases or inquiries made on your website.

- Offer to teach a class for free on your subject of expertise; include handout materials labeled with your domain name/tagline.

What about mobile tagging?

As we mentioned in Chapter 9, smartphones and other mobile devices are growing as an effective possible source of information about local pet resources in your community, and all you have to offer.

Printing a QR code or other tag on your offline materials connects your prospects immediately to your website.

Businesses reaching out to local pet parents:

- If you're placing rack cards at the local Chamber of Commerce welcome center, include a QR code that leads prospects to a special page with a discount for their first visit to you.

- You can do the same on flyers or handouts you distribute at a Family Fun Day event in your community.

- In fact, many of your printed materials can feature a QR code. Just be sure it leads people to the specific web page that's relevant to your marketing message.

Pet-industry suppliers:

- Create a direct mail piece to promote a specific product or service, include a QR code that drives readers back to a landing page that highlights key features.

- Mail key buyers a postcard with a QR code that encourages them to sign up for a free consultation.

- Add a QR code to your business card, provide prospects with more relevant information and track how many folks view the linking web page.

Last but not least, offline marketing efforts include ongoing client communications and great customer service.

If you're marketing a veterinary practice and you'd like to learn more about client communications, be sure to check out www.PfizerFrank.com, a program that trains practices on veterinarian-client-patient interactions.

If you run a retail pet supply business or service company, you may be interested in PetIndustryTV.com and other programs that provide coaching and guidance on improving customer-relations.

Make it a priority to delight your customers at all times! This can lead to fierce loyalty and free word-of-mouth advertising.

CHAPTER 12 SUMMARY/ACTION ITEMS:
Turn Offline Marketing into a Flurry of Traffic, Too!

* Offline marketing, or traditional marketing, is still a powerful part of your marketing mix.

* This category includes your organization's identity materials and other printed pieces, direct mail, radio and TV commercials, signs, trade show materials and others.

* When used alone, offline materials can bring in new visitors and profits.

* When tied into your website and mobile efforts — it can help expand your reach locally and worldwide!

* Be sure to add your website domain name to all your offline marketing efforts for various audiences.

* Also, add QR codes to campaign-specific print materials to reach people on their smartphones. Be sure the link brings them to a dedicated web page relevant to the print message.

* By combining new media/online marketing with your traditional offline marketing, you'll pack a one-two punch for sales growth.

CHAPTER 12 Additional Notes:

PART IV

Put it all together: launch and adjust for ongoing success

"I gots my green snake. Triumph!"
As Merlyn demonstrates here, there's nothing more satisfying than getting the prize —
achieving that goal you set out for yourself. It truly can happen when you know how to
take a methodical approach to your marketing in a clear, steady and easy path you can
manage and measure over time. That's what this section is about. (Green Snake Kitty
photo captured by Pam Foster)

Ta-da!

How do you feel?

Much wiser now?

Ready to conquer the marketing world?

Ready to create a brilliant marketing roadmap for success?

We certainly hope so.

This next section is the super-fun part. Now you get to pull together all your information and assemble your Profit Producing Planner; your super-clear roadmap for each week, month, quarter coming right up.

You're ready to embark on the journey you've always dreamed of — reaching more prospects in fun and easy ways, turning more of them into loyal fans, and growing your profits as a result.

Shall we?

Assemble Your Profit Producing Planner

Whee! It's time to collect all your worksheets and create your Profit Producing Planner. Each step brings you closer to finding more customers and profits.

This is where you decide which approaches to take in reaching your target prospects, and when you'll use them.

You'll create a timeline that coordinates all your marketing efforts in an easy-to-track calendar.

Don't worry! This isn't going to become a major project for you. We've made it much easier with the guidelines and worksheets in this section.

Once you complete this worksheet and combine your various marketing approaches into a checklist and timeline, your Profit Producing Planner will be a clear, detailed outline of your goals plus the steps you'll take to reach them through a carefully-selected mix of online and offline tactics.

Please remember that you're not expected to do everything all at once. We'd never advocate that anyway, because it would be impossible to do everything well and keep track of it all. It's OK and even quite smart to start with a few simple, laser-beam approaches you can measure, adjust and learn from.

In other words, use this map to include a few bright, strong flares that you shoot up into the sky, so your targeted prospects can find you amidst the wild and wooly Internet landscape!

In the following simple worksheet, you'll see that we include some mandatory marketing tactics you can't live without.

- **Brand Identity:** For example, you need to make sure your organization's identity materials professionally brand you across the board, ready to broadcast your physical location (if applicable) and website. This means adding your web domain name and tagline to as many offline/printed materials as possible. This is a must.

- **Keywords:** You'll need to have your web team research and place your best search engine keywords into your site as it's being developed, right from the start. This will help ensure that your site is found on search engines.

- **Online and offline support, back and forth:** The following checklists will help you include a terrific mix of online and offline tactics, coordinated beautifully by you so you can cast the widest net for prospects in all your audience categories, locally and across the world. We recommend selecting one or two tactics at a time and monitoring your results.

This worksheet also includes a checklist of other tactics you can add based on your comfort level, budget and resources to implement them. Again, it often makes sense to start with one or two tactics and give them your best shot before adding more.

In Chapter 14: Measure the Results, we'll discuss ways to measure the results of your marketing efforts so you can make adjustments and boost response.

Now, take a few moments to consider what goes into your Profit Producing Planner.

Select Your Marketing Mix

(Identify the specific marketing tactics you'll use to drive traffic to your site and location if applicable.)

PART 1: Overall Roadmap

Use this checklist to keep track of all your marketing efforts — both online and offline.

* When you first launch or update your website, you'll need to address all the mandatory tactics listed below to ensure the best results.

* Once your site is launched or updated, use the following list to help you include and add optional tactics as needed.

PART 2: Website usability review — MANDATORY

* **43-Point Website Usability Checklist:**
  Evaluate your current site against the best practices, and make adjustments accordingly if anything's missing or off-kilter. This should be done as soon as possible so all your other marketing efforts pay off for you!

* **Search Engine Optimization (SEO):**
  Every month, monitor and update your website's search traffic efforts based on the following findings:

  * Updated ranking report — Check in Google, Bing, MSN and Yahoo! to find out where your site ranks in search engines for various important phrases related to your business or practice.
  * Keyword adjustments — Based on your rankings in each search

engine, you may want to adjust the content of your website… or add more pages (such as articles, photos, videos, blog posts, announcements and more).

- Updated competitive analysis — Evaluate your competition's rankings to see if they've "pumped up their SEO" and are gaining ground on you… or if they're falling back.
- Updated marketing recommendations — Adjust your online strategies accordingly, for the best results.

PART 3: Online Tactics — OPTIONAL

We recommend starting with just one (or two) of these tactics to begin with, and then measuring it, tweaking it and perfecting it before moving to the next one.

- Social networks (choose one to begin with: Facebook or Twitter)
- Blogs (highly recommended)
- Videos (on your organization's own site and on your organization's YouTube channel)
- Email campaigns and/or enewsletters
- Mobile Marketing (add QR Codes to selected offline tactics listed below; create a mobile-friendly version of your site)
- Pay-Per-Click (PPC) ads
- Directory submissions
- Podcasts
- Banner ads
- Niche industry directory ads
- Linking campaigns
- Online news releases

PART 4: Offline Tactics — MANDATORY

- **Add your domain name and tagline to business identity materials:**

  - Business cards

- Letterhead sheets
- Envelopes
- Email signatures
- Promotional items
- Trade show materials
- Signs
- Answering machine and "on hold" messages
- Invoices, statements and contracts

* **Add your domain name and tagline to traditional advertising/ promotion materials:**

- Brochures, flyers and rack cards
- Sell sheets
- Newspaper ads
- Direct mail
- Radio and TV commercials
- Presentations handouts
- Media kits and press releases

PART 5: Offline Tactics — OPTIONAL

Add your domain name and tagline to other materials:
- Clothing (T-shirts, hats)
- Company vehicles
- Sponsorship materials
- Product samples (strongly recommended)
- Printed QR Codes/tags
- Other offline tactics:

_____

_____

Organize Your Marketing Efforts

First, create master lists of the marketing tactics you have tried and the results they delivered. This will help you determine what to eliminate and then add to your marketing mix.

 WORKSHEET

Master List of ONLINE Marketing Tactics you have tried

Marketing Activities	Tried Yes or No	Details	Amount Spent	Use Again
Website (site makeover strategy, if needed)				
SEO (search engine optimization)				
Social networking: Facebook				
Social networking: Twitter				
Video/YouTube				
Blogging				
PPC ads				
Banner ads				
Directory listings				
Email/Enewsletter				
Podcasts				
Linking campaign				
QR Codes				
News releases				

WORKSHEET

Master List of OFFLINE Marketing Tactics you have tried

Marketing Activities	Tried Yes or No	Details	Amount Spent	Use Again
Business cards				
Letterhead/stationery				
Envelopes				
Signs				
Answering machine "on hold" message				
Invoices, statements, contracts				
Packaging: bags, gift boxes, etc.				
Promotional items				
Other:				

WORKSHEET

Master List of ONLINE Marketing Tactics to try

Marketing Activities	Use Tactic Yes or No	Assigned To	Due By	Budget Amount	Actual Amount	Completion Date
Website (site makeover strategy, if needed)						
SEO (search engine optimization)						
Social networking: Facebook						
Social networking: Twitter						
Video/YouTube						
Blogging						
PPC ads						
Banner ads						
Directory listings						
Email/ Enewsletter						

Podcasts						
Linking campaign						
QR Codes						
News releases						

WORKSHEET

Master List of OFFLINE Marketing Tactics to try

Marketing Activities	Use Tactic Yes or No	Assigned To	Due By	Budget Amount	Actual Amount	Completion Date
Business cards						
Letterhead/ stationery						
Envelopes						
Signs						
Answering machine "on hold" message						
Invoices, statements, contracts						
Packaging: bags, gift boxes, etc.						

Promotional items						
Other:						

Marketing Activities Traditional Advertising "the classics"	Use Tactic Yes or No	Assigned To	Due By	Budget Amount	Actual Amount	Completion Date
Brochures and flyers						
Sell sheets						
Newspaper ads						
Magazine ads						
Direct mail postcards & multi-piece mailings						
Coupons, promos						
Radio commercials						
TV commercials						
Public Relations						
Media kits and press releases						

Sponsorships					
Trade shows					

Schedule it:

We highly recommend using a calendar to map out your marketing actions each day, week and each month. This 1-month example shows what you could possibly do each day.

Marketing Calendar Sample

SUNDAY	MONDAY	TUESDAY	WEDNESDAY	THURSDAY	FRIDAY	SATURDAY
	- Facebook & Twitter check - Send monthly enewsletter	- Facebook & Twitter check - Monitor LinkedIn groups -Check PPC ads	- Facebook & Twitter check - Blog post - Review previous month Google Analytics	- Facebook & Twitter check - Investigate rewards program (for retailers)	- Facebook & Twitter check - Monitor LinkedIn groups - Call vendor to create mobile app	- Facebook & Twitter check - Blog post
	- Facebook & Twitter check - Post a press release on website and submit	- Facebook & Twitter check - Monitor LinkedIn groups -Check PPC ads	- Facebook & Twitter check - Blog post - Talk with SEO expert to update competitive analysis in search	- Facebook & Twitter check - Look into a QR Code campaign	- Facebook & Twitter check - Monitor LinkedIn groups - Create How-To video	- Facebook & Twitter check - Blog post
	- Facebook & Twitter check - Post How-To video on site & YouTube	- Facebook & Twitter check - Monitor LinkedIn groups - Check PPC ads	- Facebook & Twitter check - Blog post - Prepare a direct mail postcard to target group	- Facebook & Twitter check - Send postcard to print/mail shop	- Facebook & Twitter check - Monitor LinkedIn groups - Prepare email blast for Monday	- Facebook & Twitter check - Blog post
	- Facebook & Twitter check - Send email blast	- Facebook & Twitter check - Monitor LinkedIn groups - Check PPC ads	- Facebook & Twitter check - Blog post - Discuss article plan for next month w/writer	- Facebook & Twitter check - Plan next month's How-To video	- Facebook & Twitter check - Monitor LinkedIn groups - Prepare enewsletter for Monday	- Facebook & Twitter check - Blog post

CHAPTER 13 SUMMARY/ACTION ITEMS
Assemble Your Profit Producing Planner

* Now that you've seen the most popular and effective ways to drive traffic to your physical location (if applicable) and your website, select the marketing mix you'll work with over the next several months or year.

* Some online methods will be mandatory if you want your website to succeed. Other online approaches are optional, including social media, blogging, email and more.

* Some offline methods are also mandatory for consistent branding and awareness, and then you can add optional offline approaches to round out your map.

* We recommend including a strategic mix of online and offline approaches, starting with the mandatory or "must include" methods listed in this chapter.

* Add other approaches once you've gained momentum with the first set of tactics.

* Create your Profit Producing Planner to schedule monthly marketing efforts so you can see exactly where you're going each week, month, and quarter!

CHAPTER 13 Additional Notes:

chapter

Measure and Maximize Your Marketing Results

**Easily monitor your progress and identify ways
to improve your marketing results.**

OK, here's where you get to take a look at your marketing journey's results and assess how you're doing in achieving those goals set earlier.

This step is just as important as all the others, because you need to know that your marketing efforts are working for you.

In this Chapter, we'll show you several easy ways to monitor your online and offline marketing results on a regular basis. And, we'll show you how to use this information to identify tweaks you can make to generate even more traffic and profits.

Let's begin with your website.

There are several ways to measure the results of your website's online promotions, including:

* **Your own website data**
  Each month, you can review a wealth of statistics that tell you how your site is performing. In the "traffic log report" provided online by your hosting company, you can view numbers and charts for the following:

- **Page hits** — A page hit is any request made on the web server. This includes page views, requests for images and requests for downloadable files. Caution: every single component of your pages (including individual images, charts and links) can be listed as a hit, so this is not the most realistic picture of how many unique individuals are actually visiting your site.

- **Page visits** — This is the number that tells you how many unique visitors landed on your site.

A sample Google analytics stat report is shown for review. Each hosting company may present this information differently from what you see here.

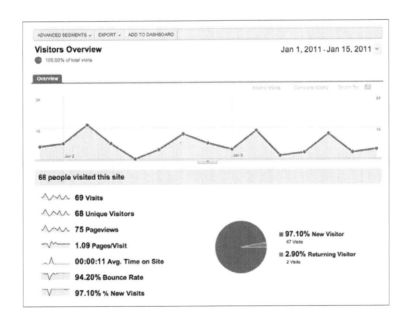

- **Search engine traffic** — This tells you which search engines (Google, Bing, Yahoo!, MSN) are referring your site to the visitors.

- **Browser traffic** — This report tells you which browsers your visitors are using (Internet Explorer, Mozilla Firefox, Netscape).

- **Bounce rate** — The percentage of bounced visits to your site. This formula indicates how fast a viewer exits your site. For example, if they enter your site and only view one page, that causes a high bounce rate. That is a bad thing. You want them to stick around and view lots of pages.

- **Your viewers' operating systems** — You can see which operating systems (Mac OS X, Microsoft Windows, Linux, etc.) your various visitors are using to view your website. This is critical so your web team can make sure your site is viewable by as many people as possible.

  CAUTION! Please ask your web team to test your site on a variety of computers using different operating systems. This will ensure that all your prospects, no matter what they use, can successfully move around your site.

- **Keywords entered** — Here's some very exciting data for you. You know how we've been telling you about the importance of key words for SEO (search engine optimization)? This keyword report will help you track the actual keywords your visitors are using in search engines… showing all the referrals in a month, broken down by the keywords that were entered.

  For example, let's say your business sells dog grooming supplies, and people have found your website by entering keywords related to this category. Your monthly stat report may list the following keywords entered into Google, in order of popularity:

Keywords	Number of entries
dog grooming supplies	1,212
dog grooming products	785

dog groomer supplies	509
dog grooming clippers	317
dog grooming tools	166
dog grooming shampoos	98

This is valuable stuff because it can help you improve your positioning in the search engines. By adjusting your site's coding and content to use the most common keywords showing up in your traffic log, more people who use these keywords will show up at your site!

To go back to the dog grooming supplies example, you might not have considered using the keywords "dog groomer supplies." You may have been focusing only on "dog grooming supplies." So, through this report, now you know that "dog groomer supplies" is also a strong keyphrase for driving traffic to your site. In fact, it's in third place according to your keyword data.

Important note: Your hosting company's traffic log isn't the only report you can use each month to review your site's overall performance. Google Analytics also provides useful tracking for anyone with a web presence.

Google Analytics provides a code that your web development team will place within your web pages. Each month, you can login and see in-depth reports that are more detailed than your average hosting company's report. For example, Google will list where people leave your site (at which page on your site), and what content on your site caught their attention. For more information and tutorials, visit www.google.com/analytics/.

Blogging

Google Analytics can also be installed on your blog to monitor much of the same information as your website. Plus, when blogging, be sure to keep track of any other sites you blog on, with their addresses. You'll see traffic that comes from those sites, too.

- **Social media efforts**

Measurements are based on the social media goals you set. For example, if you set a goal to have 1,200 fans in 3 months, monitor how many fans your marketing campaigns are generating each month and watch your social media account to see the growing number of fans.

Let's look at a report that's generated and emailed to us from Facebook, for the ATripToTheZoo.com fan page.

You'll see that it reports the number of monthly active users, how many people like us, number of wall posts and increase or decrease, plus the number of visitors — all important items you need to monitor on a monthly basis.

- **Email campaigns or enewsletters**

Your email or enewsletter campaigns can be measured in a number of ways. If you're using an online email company such as MyEmma, Mail Your Market, or Constant Contact to help automate everything (which we strongly recommend), you'll know every time you send an email:

- **How many emails were sent successfully** (the number of people who received your email/enewsletter... meaning it got through their spam filters)

- **How many emails were opened** (an industry average open rate for Entertainment category is a 15.42% open rate, according to MailChimp.com)

- **How many were bounced back to you** as a result of spam filters or people opting out of your subscriber list

- **How many people clicked-through** to the links you included in your email/enewsletter (an industry average click rate for the Entertainment category is 3.2%, according to MailChimp.com)

You may enjoy using this online email ROI calculator to see how you're doing: http://www.marketingtoday.com/tools/roi_calculator.htm.

NOTE: If you use PawsitivePerks.com/pet for your emails, they'll provide a monthly report with all this information.

Mobile Marketing

- **QR Codes and MS Tags**
Thanks to the unique code in these tags, you can track information such as:
  - How many people scanned each individual code
  - Number of scans: per hour, per day

- Types of devices being used
- Where your QR code performed best: a flyer, trade show hand out or direct mail postcard

Mobile Apps

It's important to find out how many people are downloading your apps and how often they're using them:

- Total number of times your app was downloaded from the app store
- Number of unique application users over a certain amount of time
- Active user rate — ratio of the number of app users to total number of downloads.
- How your app downloads rank compared to the industry
- The number of new users

Mobile websites

Tracking your mobile website is just as important as tracking your website. You can track the following usages: how many visitors, pages they have visited, length of stay, location and entry/exit points. Plus, you can even track the phone's model, manufacturer, service provider and language used.

Tracking the usage of your mobile site is very similar to traditional web analytics, as you'll see in these steps:

1. Clearly define what you want to track.
2. Set you budget and define how much time and money you want to devote to gathering the info. Are you going to use a free or paid service?
3. Select your service provider.
   - Google analytics, Free, www.Google.com/analytics
   - AdMob, Free, www.analytics.admob.com
   - Mixpanel, Free and paid from $50/month offers real-time analytics, www.mixpanel.com

4. Once you open your account, install (or have your web developer install) the tracking code on your mobile site.

5. Monitor results and tweak your mobile site as needed to reach your goals.

Online advertising

You can easily measure the results of your directory listing ads, banner ads, links and other online advertising. (Please note that we discuss Pay-Per-Click advertising separately below.)

For example:

- Let's say that in one month, you spent $2,000 on a banner ad located on a relevant site for your target prospects, such as the local Chamber of Commerce website.
- In that same month, you received 612 visits to your site specifically as a result of that ad.
- 57 of those visitors turned into buyers who purchased an average of $225 worth of goods or services from you.
- That's 57 x $225, which equals $12,825 in revenue. And remember, many of these customers will come back to your business if they were happy with the experience!

Now, we realize you have other costs involved in those products that were purchased, but when you compare that banner ad result to its cost, you have a winner.

Pay-Per-Click (PPC) campaigns

It's very easy to evaluate your PPC campaigns every day or month. When you set up your ads in Google, you'll use Google AdWords, which automatically provides you with reports that help you weigh the campaign costs against the results. So, all you need to do is review the report to assess:

- Number of impressions — How many times your ad comes up as a result of a search

- Number of clicks per day — Actual clicks on your ad, resulting in a visit to your site

- Average cost-per-click (CPC) — The average amount you pay each time someone clicks your ad. Average CPC is determined by totaling the cost of all clicks and dividing it by the number of clicks.

- Cost per day — This adds up all your clicks for the grand total per day

- Average ad position — Meaning 1st, 2nd, 3rd, etc. on the right-hand side of the search engine results page

- Keywords — Which targeted keywords were being typed in the most often; which generated the most responses

- You can also use Google Analytics to compare various PPC campaigns you're running and to evaluate your ROI (return on investment)

Your Public Relations efforts

This is a little tougher to figure out when it comes to measuring results, because an article or story someone saw online or in the newspaper rarely equates to a direct (measurable) response. Instead, it may be improving awareness and positive feelings about your business, which are very hard to measure.

Of course, you can look at each publication you received coverage in… their circulation, publication size, coverage placement and profile. Some measure the return on investment by considering what the equivalent exposure may have been when buying an ad. For example, if your company or practice gets a half-page profile in a magazine, and their half-page ad rate is $2,500, you received $2,500 worth of publicity.

The following 5-part process for evaluating a PR program is recommended by the Commission on PR Measurement if possible:
Source http://www.romyr.com/PRinsights/PR_effectiveness?cs_lang=en

1. Set Specific Measurable PR Goals and Objectives;
2. Measure PR Outputs (short-term results, for example, media reporting on an event);
3. Measure PR Outtakes (target group awareness after the PR program is completed);
4. Measure PR Outcomes (changes in public opinion);
5. Measure Business and/or Organizational Outcomes.

* **Your traditional sales reports**

We're assuming you already track new contacts and leads for your products or services, as well as actual sales for your programs and products. As you launch or re-launch your website pages, you'll want to set up new entries in your sales tracking system to include leads and sales that come into your organization as a result of your website.

You can do this by tracking inquiries that come to you via your site's Contact Form and Enewsletter sign-up form, as well as actual sales that come to you via your shopping cart (if you sell supplies in an ecommerce store).

What about offline marketing results?

You'll notice that we haven't mentioned your offline marketing efforts in this Step. Many of the offline strategies will not be directly measurable. For example, it's absolutely necessary to include your domain name on all your business identity materials, but you won't be able to equate that directly with an increase in website traffic or visits.

One way you can track the outcome of your offline efforts is by creating a direct marketing postcard, print ad, TV spot or radio commercial that drives prospects to a specific landing page or promotion on your site. You'll see an increase in website hits that tell you the direct marketing campaign was a winner … as long as your landing page is set up properly to drive click-throughs and purchases!

We've just shown you dozens of ways to measure your marketing efforts and this could be overwhelming. But — we're here to help!

To keep track of all your online and offline results, we're providing the following helpful checklist.

The Marketing Measurement Checklist

Each month, monitor your marketing results to evaluate effectiveness.

1. **Your own website data**

    Traffic log report from your hosting company and/or Google Analytics:
    Page hits: _____
    Page visits: _____
    Total unique visitors: _____
    Number of new visitors: _____
    Pages viewed: _____
    Number of pages visited per visit: _____
    Duration on each page: _____
    Browser types: _____
    Bounce rate: _____
    Operating systems: _____

Referring domains: _____

Keywords entered: (list in order, starting with most frequent) _____

_____

2. Social media efforts

Facebook:

Number of Facebook fans: _____ + or - since last week _____

Number of monthly active users: _____ + or - since last week_____

Number of wall posts this week:_____ + or - since last week_____

Number of visits this week:_____+ or - since last week _____

Twitter:

Number of Twitter fans:_____

Number of Retweets:_____

Number of Mentions:_____

3. Emails/Enewsletters

Number sent successfully: _____

Number opened: _____

Number bounced back: _____

Number of click-throughs on links:_____

4. Mobile Marketing

Track QR codes & MS Tags

Campaign name: _____

Number of scans: _____

    per hour: _____

    per day: _____

Type of devices used to scan: _____

Mobile Apps

Total numbers of apps downloaded this month:_____

Number of unique app users this month: _____

Active user rate this month:_____

App ranking compared to industry: _____

Mobile website

Number of visitors:_____

Pages they have visited:_____

Length of stay:_____

Location and entry/exit points:_____

Plus, track the phone's model, manufacturer, service provider and language used: _____

5. General online advertising

Banner ad click-throughs to your landing page:_____

Inquiries or purchases as a result: _____

Directory listing click-throughs to your landing page: _____

Inquiries or purchases as a result: _____

6. Pay-Per-Click (PPC) campaigns Google AdWords report:

Number of impressions:_____

Number of clicks per day:_____

Average cost per click: _____

Cost per day (total clicks):_____

Average ad position:_____

Targeted keywords:_____

7. Link-building campaigns

Number of sites linking to yours:_____

URLs of sites linking to yours:_____

_____

8. Public Relations

Monitor each PR campaign

PR outputs:_____

PR outtakes:_____

9. Your traditional sales reports

Inquiries received via Contact Form:_____

Leads via Enewsletter Sign-up Form:_____

Purchases made via shopping cart: _____

A final comment on your marketing efforts.

It's a commitment to an ongoing process.

There are millions of web pages on the Internet, and the odds of people finding you are not very good unless you plan to make a REGULAR effort to reach your prospects and customers.

Even if you're able to get your site indexed on page 1 of the search engine results, your site can drop in ranking if your web pages don't stay fresh or you don't add new content on a regular basis. In addition, your indexing can change because search engine algorithms continually change or your competition could have become a smarter web marketer.

Therefore, to maintain and even improve your rankings, you must optimize your pages, monitor your rankings and continue to fine-tune them as needed. And, you need to commit to frequently trying some search engine marketing campaigns mixed in with other marketing efforts.

In other words, your online marketing efforts should become an integral component of your overall marketing plan each year, with a clear path and schedule that you follow weekly or at least monthly for effective, lasting results that continually grow your profits!

CHAPTER 14 SUMMARY/ACTION ITEMS:
Measure and Maximize Your Results

* Luckily, your web marketing efforts can be very easily measured. A number of reports and statistics can show you exactly how you're doing each month.

* Your hosting company provides you with a "traffic log report" online to show you the number of people visiting your site, what keywords they're using, and what search engines referred them to you.

* Google Analytics is another great tool for evaluating your web response numbers.

* Your online advertising is also very easy to measure. You'll receive detailed reports on the activity of your banner ads, directory listing ads, etc.

* Pay-Per-Click advertising results can be measured daily, which is great because you'll know immediately if an ad is working and which keywords are getting the best response.

* Emails and enewsletters are also easy to track if you use an online contact management program such as MyEmma.com, MailYourMarket.com, MailChimp.com or ConstantContact.com. They provide detailed reports at any time.

* Your own sales monitoring systems will also tell you how it's going, because you can track inquiries and sales that come in from your website.

* Once you evaluate all the results information, you can adjust your keywords, change your banner ads, test other offers in your PPC ads, and make other changes that could boost results — and profits — even more.

CHAPTER 14 Additional Notes:

Conclusion

Give yourself a round of applause! You've arrived at your beautiful new marketing water dish, and now you can drink in all the cool knowledge you've gained.

Now you know what only about 35% of web marketers know. Doesn't it feel great?

Let's recap what you're learned as a result of diving into this guide and tackling all the planning tools we've provided you.

* You've learned about 17 years' worth of web success rules, usability guidelines and best practices, all boiled down to clear essentials you need today.

* You understand how to attract the right prospects to your business or practice... and how to get them excited about your products and services.

* You know enough online marketing terminology to intelligently discuss your needs and purpose with a professional web and marketing team, so they'll do a great job for you.

* You're armed with a clear action guide, a set of interview questions and a number of checklists that will help you tackle some of these steps yourself and also find the best team to help you build a profitable marketing approach.

❧ And best of all, you're ready to dive in and try some exciting new ways to bring more visitors and dollars to your organization… and then track your success!

CONGRATULATIONS!

If you haven't completed all the Appendix worksheets yet, it will be well worth your time to do so. Once you're done, you'll have a complete Profit Producing Planner for success.

We wish you the best of luck and success in your venture. Please let us know how it goes!

Email us at info@PawzoolaPublishing.com with your stories and domain names.

And, if you ever wish to contact us and discuss your specific website concerns, we're available for consultations, workshops, seminars, training, site assessments, research, site audits, web-SEO content writing and other services. We'd also like your feedback on the usefulness of this guide.

Please contact us at info@PawzoolaPublishing.com.

We promise to get right back to you.

Here's to your marketing success ~
Pam and C S

About the Authors

Who are these friendly marketing guides, dedicated to your success?

Pam Foster
PetCopywriter.com
NAVC (North American Veterinary Community)
Certified SEO Copywriter and Web Consultant

Pam is an experienced web copywriter and sales catalyst who specializes in writing strategic marketing copy that turns prospects into qualified, eager sales leads and customers for her clients' businesses.

Her diverse 31-year copywriting background includes pet companies, veterinary manufacturing companies, biotechnology, veterinary care, nonprofit, small business, direct response, supplemental education and much more. Clients have included LifeLearn, MyPetEd.com, IDEXX Laboratories, DirectVetMarketing, PetAmberAlert.com and many other pet and veterinary companies.

Pam is uniquely strategic and results-driven, helping clients determine the best way to reach their target audiences and achieve their sales and lead-generation goals. She has written for every type of marketing media there is, with 15 years of experience in web content writing, SEO, web content makeovers, direct response, enewsletters and email/landing page testing.

Pam shares C S's lifelong passion for pets and animals of all types. Her family has included dogs and cats throughout her life, and her father and stepmother managed a farm in Maine where cats, goats, sheep, ducks, geese and even guinea hens resided at various times.

Some of Pam's earlier animal memories include lambs running around the kitchen every spring, and frequent trips to Simpson's Animal Farm to feed swans and enjoy the petting zoo. Her days of riding with her father and sister in the "Swan boat" are treasured memories. More recently, Pam enjoyed swimming with dolphins in the Florida Keys and she was thrilled to finally visit the San Diego Zoo in 2011.

During her time as a catalog copywriter at L.L. Bean, Pam was in charge of writing about the dog beds and other pet-related products. Just after that, from 2000 to 2006, she worked at the veterinary diagnostics company IDEXX Laboratories, This was where Pam became immersed in learning about animal care and helping veterinarians find diagnostic solutions that supported quicker answers and successful treatment. Pam worked side-by-side with veterinary practices and scientists to create materials that showcased the latest technologies for care.

In 2006, after several years of working in corporate America, Pam launched her freelance copywriting and consulting business and worked for a wide variety of companies. She also worked for The Pet Health Network, a startup organization that supplied an innovative touch-screen education technology to veterinarians, helping them explain medical procedures to pet owners.

In 2010, Pam turned her focus to pet and veterinary marketing, establishing PetCopywriter.com, and today she works with a growing number of animal-related businesses.

Since then, she has devoted most of her efforts to helping companies that market to pet owners, pet companies, veterinary practices, horse owners and other animal-related audiences. She works as a virtual team member with web developers, graphic designers and others to launch websites, optimize existing sites, and help test email and landing page campaigns.

"Pam is a top notch copywriter. She's able to synthesize veterinary information into terms that consumers can easily understand. Pam is not afraid to challenge ideas and assumptions, which in a small team brings tremendous value. I highly recommend Pam." — Larry Chasse, DirectVet Marketing

Pam's work has generated countless leads and sales, and has been recognized with more than 100 awards from national and regional organizations including New England DMA (Direct Marketing Association), Web Marketing Association, Telly, *Catalog Age,* League of American Communications Professionals and American Inhouse Design.

She enjoys teaching, speaking and training, and is a frequent speaker and trainer for LifeLearn and AWAI, presenting guidance on topics that include online marketing, niche marketing, SEO and social media. She's also a guest columnist for Veterinary Advantage magazine.

Pam's professional affiliations include American Writers & Artists Inc. (Founders Circle member, Wall of Fame Recipient and 2009 $10K Challenge Honoree) and the Women in the Pet Industry Association. Visit www.PetCopywriter.com for more details on Pam's skills, services and background.

Pam is now the Managine Editor, Community Content and Media for the NAVC, a nonprofit organization in the veterinary industry. She currently lives in Jacksonville, Florida, where she and her dog Louie are surrounded by glorious dolphins and other southern wildlife.

For web and SEO consulting, copywriting, speaking, training and other services, you can reach Pam at:
Phone: 843-597-6515
Email: pam@petcopywriter.com

Pam is co-founder of www.PawzoolaPublishing.com.

C S Wurzberger
WildlyProfitableMarketing.com
TheGreenUpGirl.com
ATriptotheZoo.com

C S Wurzberger, aka, The Green Up Girl is an accomplished sustainability consultant and marketing strategist with over 25 years of experience.

With a specialized focus on helping pet-related and eco-friendly businesses promote their products and services with the goal of attracting more customers. C S helps clients assess their current sustainability and marketing issues and maps out their strategies for success.

C S is well versed in the animal niche as a former owner of a Llama touring company, owner/operator of a summer camp for children and director of a 150-acre, 300-animal USDA- licensed petting zoo.

Her zoo and animal park focus started when she was 7 years old and her parents took her to the Catskill Game Farm, formally located in upstate New York. She was so excited to be at the zoo. As a young child, she was enthralled with animals and spent most of her waking moments reading and exploring the animal world. While at the Catskill Game Farm, she spent her time running from exhibit to exhibit, gazing at each animal with amazement, reading every sign and trying so hard to memorize each and every fact.

Then suddenly she saw this lady behind the bear cage, with a big key chain. She asked her mom, who was that? Her mom answered, "That lady is a zoo keeper. She's in charge of feeding and caring for the animals." As C S watched further, the lady unlocked the cage and dropped in the bear's food. Wow, at that exact moment, C S knew she wanted to be the person with all THE KEYS TO THE ZOO when she grew up.

Before that dream came to life… C S worked with her father and managed their Country Store in Wilmington, Vermont, was the owner of a Llama touring company called "Llunch with a Llama," owner of a tack shop selling equestrian supplies and then she traveled Northern New England as a sales representative in the gift and toy industry.

Then C S, her 7-year-old daughter, 4 horses, 2 llamas, 2 cats, 2 bunnies, and 2 dogs packed up and move to Portland, Maine to become the director of a 150-acre, 300-animal, USDA-licensed petting zoo, where she created, implemented and marketed their educational programs. (C S is also an avid equestrian and has been riding since she was 2 years old — western pleasure and hunt seat — and trained with some top folks through the years: Sally Swift, Linda Tellington-Jones, John Lyons, to name a few.)

After the owner of the petting zoo retired and closed the zoo, C S went back to school to study web design and Internet marketing. She and her team have assisted hundreds of folks from around the world to build and market profitable, successful websites that rank high in the search engines.

One of C S's passions is teaching and sharing information, and she's an in-demand web educator. C S shares her real-world expertise with a variety of business organizations devoted to small-business success, including SCORE® Counselors to America's Businesses, several professional organizations including Center for Women and Enterprise, Boston, national gift shows across the country, including the National Stationery show, NYC, Boston Gift Show, Halloween & Costume show, Chicago, Transworld exhibit's Variety and Gift Show and educational institutions such as Simmons School of Management, Boston and MBA instructor for Interise, Boston. Plus serves on the board of Magical Earth Retreats; a place where children and adults reconnect with Mother Nature.

Even with her love and devotion of teaching and marketing businesses, something was missing. Her soul was missing the animal world. Deep down she really wanted her life to stand for more, She wanted to make a difference in the world. Her soul wanted to connect people with animals from around the world.

Hence… THE DREAM… www.ATripToTheZoo.com, www.ZooMarketingTools.com/pet and www.TheGreenUpGirl.com were born.

With passion and purpose, she leads a team that connects people who love animals with great zoos, aquariums and conservation centers from around the world. As part of their mission, they lend a helping paw by giving back 20% of their profits to rescue and conservation centers.

This is her work:
* Promoting zoos, aquariums, nature centers and animal-related locations from around the world in her directory ATripToThe Zoo.com so they can attract more visitors.
* Presenting seminars and workshops at conferences, trade shows and individual locations.
* Promoting conservation programs that are instrumental in helping our animals around the world survive and thrive.
* Raising awareness and teaching people about the endangered animals we share the earth with.
* Teaching children about endangered animals, both in-person and through the sale of activity kits.
* Inspiring people to enjoy a greener lifestyle while connecting them with recycled, natural and organic products.

- Presenting marketing and how-to green up seminars and workshops at conferences, trade shows and individual locations.

In 2012, C S earned her Masters Certificate in Sustainable Innovation from the University of Vermont.

C S's daughter is now grown and has twin 5-year-old boys. C S lives in Wilmington, Vermont, where you will find her hiking the mountains, kayaking, horseback riding, and doing anything else that involves nature and the outdoors. Plus, you'll find her traveling the country, visiting zoos, aquariums, nature centers and writing her Blog.

For marketing consulting, speaking, training and other services, contact C S at 802-258-8046 or CS@TheGreenUpGirl.com

C S is co-founder of www.PawzoolaPublishing.com.

Appendix

Worksheets, Checklists and Resources
for Your Profit Producing Planner

Most of the chapters in our book include worksheets or checklists that help you organize your marketing mission, goals and tactics. While those worksheets are fine in context of each chapter's topic and discussion, we know it's helpful to have a clean set to work with, all in one place.

Here, you can use these blank templates to put it together your Profit Producing Planner.

Each worksheet and checklist in this section represents an important piece of your focused marketing guide — a clear reference point for action.

These worksheets and checklists are also available at www.PawzoolaPublishing.com as 8½" x 11" sheets you can download and work with. You may want to fill them in, print them out and put them in a notebook for easy reference at any time.

If you get stuck, we're always a phone call or email away. We can set up a time for a personal consultation or training if it will help bring this home for you.

Also visit www.PawzoolaPublishing.com for other guidance, training materials, how-to-workshops and webinars.
Woo-hoo! Enjoy.

Pam and C S
info@PawzoolaPublishing.com

Worksheets and checklists included in this section:

- Define Your Ultimate Destination (Chapter 1)
- Competitor Evaluation Sheet (individual) (Chapter 2)
- Competition Master Sheet (comparing several competitors) (Chapter 2)
- Know Your Target Audience: Prospect/Persona Question List (Chapter 3)
- 43-Point Website Usability Checklist (Chapter 4)
- Your Site Map (Wireframe/Architecture Template) (Chapter 4)
- Web Creative Brief (Chapter 4)
- Web Team Interview Questionnaire (Chapter 5)
- Keyword Research Checklist (Chapter 6)
- Online Tactics Checklist – tactics you have tried (Chapter 13)
- Offline Tactics Checklist – tactics you have tried (Chapter 13)
- Online Tactics Checklist – tactics to try (Mandatory and Optional) (Chapter 13)
- Offline Tactics Checklist – tactics to try (Mandatory and Optional) (Chapter 13)
- Calendar (1 quarter example to get started) (Chapter 13)
- Measuring Checklist/Sheet (Chapter 14)

Define your Ultimate Destination

(Confirm Your Business Mission and Unique Value)

Part 1: Company Information

Organization name: _____

Marketing contact name: _____

Address: _____

City: _____ State: _____ Zip: _____

Phone: _____ Fax: _____ Cell: _____

Website Address (URL): _____

Email Address: _____

# of years in business: ____ # of employees: ____ # of customers: ____

Describe what makes your business special or different, in 4 sentences or less.
For example, what sights, sounds, feelings, outcomes and other experiences do you offer that your audience may not find anywhere else?

Where are you now:

What types of products, services and solutions do you offer?
[Example: all-natural dog food and treats, a website with luxury pet supplies, a membership/rewards program, training services, grooming services, pet cleaning supplies, innovative medical solutions, etc.]

How's business? Describe your current business climate. (What are the trends? What's popular?) [Example: Organic and natural pet food sales are expected to grow 3 times as fast as pet food sales overall through 2015 (Packaged Facts data).]

Describe your current market position in your geographic region if you depend on local business. (Where do you currently stand?) [Example: There are 3 major pet supply stores that compete for pet-parent dollars. People don't think to come to our boutique pet supply store more than once every few weeks or months.]

What barriers do you have to overcome — what might stop pet parents from visiting your retail store, doggie daycare, grooming facility or website… or what might stop pet companies or veterinary practices from buying your solutions? [Example: There are many competitors in our territory or market category, or potential visitors can't find our website in the search engines, etc.]

What makes your products or services unique or special in the buying landscape? What's the biggest benefit or unique solution you offer customers or target prospects? [Example: Of all the leash and collar companies selling products online, ours is the only one offering hand-tooled leather products that can be personalized with the pet's name and other finishing touches such as chrome accents.]

What were your organization's top 3 accomplishments during the last year regarding business growth?

What were the top 3 growth challenges your organization faced last year?

What did your organization fail to achieve last year with its marketing?

Clarify your business vision — what drives your current sales and your future:

* What types of programs, experiences, products and/or services do you really want to provide and promote?

* What is your organization's history?

* Where do you want your revenue and position to be at the end of the year? (In other words, what's your biggest marketing wish for the coming year?)

❧ What are your primary marketing goals? Let's get super-specific by setting 3 to 6 [S.M.A.R.T.] marketing objectives to grow your company. They need to be:
  - Specific
  - Measurable
  - Actionable
  - Realistic
  - Time-based

  Example: Increase monthly sales 12% within the next 12 months, or sell 125 widgets this month.

Now set your yearly marketing objectives:

1.

2.

3.

4.

5.

Competitor Evaluation Sheet

Competitor (Other pet businesses or veterinary practices in your community and/or online):

Business name: _____

Marketing contact name: _____

Address: _____

City: _____ State: _____ Zip: _____

Phone: _____ Fax: _____ Cell: _____

Website Address (URL): _____

Email Address: _____

# of years in business: _____ # of employees: _____ # of customers: _____

Brief description of their business:

List their primary products/services | and prices

_____ | _____

_____ | _____

_____ | _____

_____ | _____

_____ | _____

What do they offer that's similar to your business?

What do they offer that's unique or different from your business?

What are their strengths? | What are their weaknesses?

_____ | _____

_____ | _____

_____ | _____

_____ | _____

_____ | _____

On a scale of 1-10, how user-friendly is their website?

Competition Master Sheet

Now, collect your competitor worksheets and fill in the following table to compare your business to your local (if applicable) and online competitors.

	YOUR COMPANY	COMPETITOR #1	COMPETITOR #2	COMPETITOR #3
PRODUCTS OR SERVICES				
PRICES				
TARGET CUSTOMERS				
MARKET POSITION				
MARKETING TACTICS				
TAGLINE OR SLOGAN				

Know Your Target Audience
(Define the Searchers You're Trying to Attract)

Here are the key questions that help you better understand your ideal prospects:

* **What types of people or businesses are you trying to attract to your organization's various offerings?** [List everything you can about them: gender, age, geographic location, etc.]

* **What are their characteristics?** [List their lifestyles, buying habits, hobbies, etc.]

* **Are they sophisticated, knowledgeable consumers regarding your offerings… or do you need to educate them?** [For example, do they already use all the items or services you offer or are you breaking new ground with them?]

* **What do you know about their interests, attitudes, hopes and needs — especially related to your various offerings?** [For example, are they excited about your products or services… or had they not even considered them?]

* **What major "pain" or need do they have that your organization can alleviate or address (what keeps them up at night)?** This will

be different for each target: pet parents, pet-supply store owners, veterinary practices, etc. [For example, someone with an aging dog is hoping to ease their pet's aching joints and maintain a good quality of life in the golden years.]

* **What solution are they looking for?** [For example, are they looking for something that's easier, cheaper, faster; or something that will make them be a hero by keeping their pets healthy and happy? To be specific as possible, go back to page 19 to review the examples of what searchers are looking for.]

* **How do your products or services offer the BEST solution for these prospects?** [For example, is it the easiest, cheapest, fastest, most reliable, most attractive or meaningful solution? This is where it really pays to know your competition and what they offer.]

Our 43-Point Checklist for
Your Web Marketing Excellence

Site identity:

☐ 1. Show your organization's name and logo in the upper left-hand corner or at least in the top masthead area.

☐ 2. Include a tagline that summarizes the main benefit your business or organization offers in a customer-focused benefit statement (such as, "The Original High-Density Foam Pet Ramps and Steps" as shown).

☐ 3. Include a marketing hook (headline) that emphasizes your organization's unique value and solutions from the visitor's point of view.

Company information:

☐ 4. Include an "About Us" page with location or company information.

☐ 5. Organize your information into standard/expected categories, such as:

- Our Staff
- Press Room
- History

☐ 6. Present a unified face/brand to your audiences. All web pages and related marketing materials include your organization's brand look and "voice." (Everything needs to look like brothers and sisters.)

☐ 7. Include a "Contact Us" button that goes to a page with all contact information: email, phone and physical address, as well as live chat or other contact features.

☐ 8. Include a footer on every page with:

- Organization name
- Address
- Phone
- Live link to email

☐ 9. If your site gathers customer information, include a "Privacy Policy" page.

Content:

☐ 10. Use customer-focused language that explains the benefits of your business: what's in it for the visitor. Explain how you provide solutions or services in a way no one else offers. Or, if you're a supplier, show the special benefits of doing business with you.

☐ 11. Incorporate keywords into content in ethical, well-crafted messages, especially in the headline, subhead and other main areas. (See Chapter 6.)

☐ 12. Use "benefit-rich" bullets that make the content easy to scan.

☐ 13. Use uppercase letters sparingly for easier reading.

Links:

☐ 14. Differentiate links and make them stand out through bold and/or underline format (underlines are especially helpful for vision-impaired individuals). The only exception is your Social Sharing links. (See Point #42.)

☐ 15. Don't use generic instructions, such as "Click here," as a link name. Use specific beneficial action words instead, such as "Find your lost pet now."

☐ 16. Allow link colors to show visited and unvisited status, so your visitors remember whether or not they clicked on the link already. (Standard link colors: Blue #0000FF visitor has not been to yet, Purple #800080 visited link, Red #FF0000 active link)

☐ 17. If a link goes to a non-web page item such as a PDF, video clip, audio clip, email window, etc., add an icon or short caption indicating this so there are no surprises for the visitor.

Navigation:

☐ 18. Make sure your primary navigation runs across the top of the page or down the left, never on the right. Reader studies prove that visitors expect your buttons to be placed in these locations for a user-friendly experience.

☐ 19. Group similar items together within navigation sections.

☐ 20. Use standard naming conventions: Home, About Us, Products, Services, Directions, Contact Us. Don't use made-up words for button names; it may confuse visitors.

☐ 21. If you sell products on your website, place the shopping cart buttons in the upper right-hand side of the main masthead so people see it on every page. The most popular button names are:

- Your account
- Shopping cart
- Check out

☐ 22. Add a site map, which helps visitors and search engines know what's on your website.

Search boxes within your site: If you offer a search function on your site...

☐ 23. Give users a SEARCH box on the home page (so they can

quickly find what they are looking for), not a link to a search page.

☐ 24. Use a "search" or "go" button to the right of the box.

☐ 25. Don't offer a "search the web" feature. In general, don't link people to other websites. Why would you want visitors to leave your site?

Graphics and animation:

☐ 26. Optimize graphics to web-appropriate sizes (72 dpi is recommended). Be aware that large files slow down page viewing and annoy visitors. (In fact, search engines punish slow-loading sites.)

☐ 27. Use photos that relate to the content, not just as decorations or irrelevant entertainment.

☐ 28. Let users choose whether they want to see an animated intro to your site! Don't make it the default.

☐ 29. Video and audio should be in the off position. Give users the option of turning them on with a clear PLAY button. Even better, offer a MUTE button for the sound.

Graphic design:

☐ 30. Limit font styles to 2 or 3 maximum per site. Over-designing the site can be distracting to the user.

☐ 31. Use black type on a white background for easy reading... especially for the body text where there's lots of copy.

☐ 32. Avoid forcing visitors to do horizontal (side-by-side) scrolling at 800 x 600 screen size.

☐ 33. The most critical page elements should be visible "above the fold" — on the first screen visitors see when they land on your web pages. (Above the fold is a graphic term that refers to placing graphics in the upper half of the web page.)

☐ 34. Make sure pages rarely force the visitor to scroll more than 2.2 times. (Exception: sales-letter landing pages.)

☐ 35. Avoid using pop-up windows. Yes, some companies swear by them. But most web visitors find them to be distracting and annoying. (A recent study identified them as one of the "top hated" online marketing techniques.)

Communicating unfinished pages:

☐ 36. If parts of your website are not finished, add a date of when they will be finished. (Statistics show that when a viewer goes to a page under construction you have a 12% chance of having that person come back to your site. Yuck.)

SEO (search engine optimization) basics (we cover SEO in detail in Chapter 6):

Make sure every page of your site includes these unique and relevant behind-the-scenes "meta tags":

☐ 37. Title tag with keywords/keyphrases. (70 characters/spaces maximum; real sentences are best)

☐ 38. Header tags with keywords/keyphrases. (Headline = H1 Tag, Subhead = H2 Tag)

☐ 39. Meta description using keywords/keyphrases in a complete sentence or two (this may be displayed in search engines; limit to 150 characters/spaces)

☐ 40. Keyword tag. (Ideally no more than 10 keyword phrases)

☐ 41. Alt tags with keywords/keyphrases. (for charts, photos and other graphics that aren't text)

Social Media:

☐ 42. Place your social media buttons/links prominently at the top of each page (see the Red Bank Veterinary Hospital example). Or, in the upper part of your right-hand margin. Also, invite people to join you and share any benefits they may receive as a follower.

☐ 43. Include an invitation to subscribe to your blog by email and/or RSS feed, and also to share posts in social media. The best placement is also in the upper right part of your right-hand column.

Your Site Map Wireframe/Architecture Template

Sample Sitemap for a Pet Services Business

Main Navigation

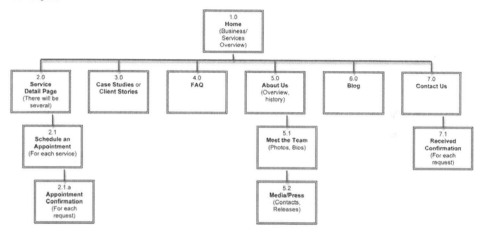

The Web Creative Brief

(Identify the critical design elements and key messages for your site.)

PART 1: Current Situation

* Business marketing goals:

* Competitive climate:

* Barriers to overcome — what might stop customers from buying? (price, not aware, selection)

* What marketing efforts have worked? Not worked?

PART 2: Graphic Design Considerations

* What does your current brand look like? Describe in detail (or attach your Branding Guidelines):

* Logo:

* Color palette:

* Typography (fonts and styles):

* Imagery (illustration, art):

* Photography:

* Other considerations (use of white space, position of elements): What is the visual tone to be conveyed on your site? (light-hearted, fun, practical, bright, cheery, serious, authoritative, feminine)

- Does your audience already know your brand?

- What do your competitors look like on their sites?

- Do you own digital photographs for your products, services and people? If so, in what size and format?

- Do you own artwork/illustrations?

PART 3: Content/Message Considerations:

- What's the main UNIQUE benefit or solution only your facility, products and services can offer? (This is the USP, or Unique Selling Proposition/Unique Solution Proposition.)

- List the key features of your organization: what you offer.

- List the key benefits of your organization: the desired results or value of what you offer.

- How interested is the target audience in your events, products and solutions?

- What key "pains" of your target audience (problems or wishes), can you solve?

- What are you really selling? (e.g., you're not selling pet portraits/photography; you're selling a special image/heirloom that honors a beloved pet. Or, you're not selling innovative diagnostic blood analyzers to veterinarians; you're selling better medical answers so the practitioner can be a hero to his clients.)

- Are there any other emotional motivators you should consider (frustration, pride, greed)?

- What support or "reasons to believe" do you have for your key promise messages (testimonials, endorsements, case studies, product specifics, etc.)?

- What obstacles or objections do you need to overcome for success?

- What are your competitors offering?

- How can you set your business or organization apart from the competition? Why choose you?

- What's the proper, branded tone of "voice" for your messages? (serious, light-hearted, fun, practical)

- Does your audience know you? Will you need to address issues of credibility?

- What phrases (keywords) does your audience use to find your products or services in search engines... or what would you expect them to use?

- What is your call-to-action? Why should the audience respond NOW?

- How can the audience respond to you (phone/mail/web/mail/fax)?

Web Team Interview Questionnaire
Hire the best crew you can afford

To get a true sense of what a professional web team can do for you, use these interview questions when you meet with the various candidates:

* What are your credentials?

* What is your site domain? (Take a look at the candidate's site to see if it follows the best practices we've outlined in Chapter 4.)

* What are your technical capabilities?

* What skills and training do you have?

* Can you provide samples of your work — sites that are optimized, profitable and successful?

* Do you have any before/after screen shots, case studies, or other proof of your work results?

* Can you describe your web development process?

* Can you explain your process and its phases in non-technical terms so I can understand and make smart decisions?

* What's the average budget range you work with?

* Will you turn over ownership of all graphics created for my site?

* Would you please provide references from at least 3 satisfied clients?

Keyword Research Checklist

1. Make a list of all the keywords you can think of for each web page:

_____   _____

_____   _____

_____   _____

2. Keywords from customer interviews:

_____   _____

_____   _____

_____   _____

3. Keywords from your traffic reports:

_____   _____

_____   _____

_____   _____

4. Keywords from your competition:

Competitor 1:

_____   _____

_____   _____

_____   _____

Competitor 2:

_____   _____

_____   _____

_____   _____

Competitor 3:

_____   _____

_____   _____

_____   _____

5. Cover all keyword variations:

_____   _____

_____   _____

_____   _____

6. Be descriptive:

_____   _____

_____   _____

_____   _____

7. Use action words:

_____   _____

_____   _____

_____   _____

8. Target local markets, if relevant:

_____   _____

_____   _____

_____   _____

9. Keywords from research tools:

_____   _____

_____   _____

_____   _____

10. Keyword placement:

Page: _____ Keywords: _____

Page: _____ Keywords: _____

Page: _____ Keywords: _____

Page: _____ Keywords: _____

Page: _____ Keywords: _____

ONLINE Marketing Tactics You Have Tried

Marketing Activities	Tried Yes or No	Details	Amount Spent	Use Again
Website (site makeover strategy, if needed)				
SEO (search engine optimization)				
Social networking: Facebook				
Social networking: Twitter				
Video/YouTube				
Blogging				
PPC ads				
Banner ads				
Directory listings				
Email/Enewsletter				
Podcasts				
Linking campaign				
QR Codes				
News releases				

OFFLINE Marketing Tactics You Have Tried

Marketing Activities	Tried Yes or No	Details	Amount Spent	Use Again
Business cards				
Letterhead/stationery				
Envelopes				
Signs				
Answering machine "on hold" message				
Invoices, statements, contracts				
Packaging: bags, gift boxes, etc.				
Promotional items				
Other:				

ONLINE Marketing Tactics To Try

Marketing Activities	Use Tactic Yes or No	Assigned To	Due By	Budget Amount	Actual Amount	Completion Date
Website (site makeover strategy, if needed)						
SEO (search engine optimization)						
Social networking: Facebook						
Social networking: Twitter						
Video/YouTube						
Blogging						
PPC ads						
Banner ads						
Directory listings						
Email/ Enewsletter						
Podcasts						

ONLINE Marketing Tactics To Try (cont'd)

Linking campaign						
QR Codes						
News releases						

OFFLINE Marketing Tactics To Try

Marketing Activities	Use Tactic Yes or No	Assigned To	Due By	Budget Amount	Actual Amount	Completion Date
Business cards						
Letterhead/ stationery						
Envelopes						
Signs						
Answering machine "on hold" message						
Invoices, statements, contracts						
Packaging: bags, gift boxes, etc.						
Promotional items						
Other:						

OFFLINE Marketing Tactics To Try (cont'd)

Marketing Activities Traditional Advertising "the classics"	Use Tactic Yes or No	Assigned To	Due By	Budget Amount	Actual Amount	Completion Date
Brochures and flyers						
Sell sheets						
Newspaper ads						
Magazine ads						
Direct mail postcards & multi-piece mailings						
Coupons, promos						
Radio commercials						
TV commercials						
Public Relations						
Media kits and press releases						
Sponsorships						
Trade shows						

Marketing Calendar

Map out your marketing actions each week/month/year

SUNDAY	MONDAY	TUESDAY	WEDNESDAY	THURSDAY	FRIDAY	SATURDAY

The Marketing Measurement Checklist

Each month, monitor your marketing results to evaluate effectiveness.

1. Your own website data

Traffic log report from your hosting company and/or Google Analytics:

Page hits: _____

Page visits: _____

Total unique visitors: _____

Number of new visitors:_____

Pages viewed:_____

Number of pages visited per visit:_____

Duration on each page:_____

Browser types:_____

Bounce rate:_____

Operating systems:_____

Referring domains: _____

Keywords entered: (list in order, starting with most frequent) _____

2. Social media efforts

Facebook:

Number of Facebook fans: _____ + or - since last week _____

Number of monthly active users: _____ + or - since last week_____

Number of wall posts this week:_____ + or - since last week_____

Number of visits this week:_____+ or - since last week _____

Twitter:

Number of Twitter fans: _____

Number of Retweets: _____

Number of Mentions: _____

3. Emails/Enewsletters

Number sent successfully: _____

Number opened: _____

Number bounced back: _____

Number of click-throughs on links: _____

4. Mobile Marketing

Track QR codes & MS Tags

Campaign name: _____

Number of scans: _____

    per hour: _____

    per day: _____

Type of devices used to scan: _____

Mobile Apps

Total numbers of apps downloaded this month: _____

Number of unique app users this month: _____

Active user rate this month: _____

App ranking compared to industry: _____

Mobile website

Number of visitors: _____

Pages they have visited: _____

Length of stay: _____

Location and entry/exit points: _____

Plus, track the phone's model, manufacturer, service provider and language used: _____

5. General online advertising

Banner ad click-throughs to your landing page:_____

Inquiries or purchases as a result: _____

Directory listing click-throughs to your landing page:_____

Inquiries or purchases as a result: _____

6. Pay-Per-Click (PPC) campaigns Google AdWords report:

Number of impressions: _____

Number of clicks per day:_____

Average cost per click: _____

Cost per day (total clicks): _____

Average ad position: _____

Targeted keywords: _____

7. Link-building campaigns

Number of sites linking to yours:_____

URLs of sites linking to yours: _____

_____

8. Public Relations

Monitor each PR campaign

PR outputs:_____

PR outtakes:_____

9. Your traditional sales reports

Inquiries received via Contact Form: _____

Leads via Enewsletter Sign-up Form: _____

Purchases made via shopping cart: _____

Marketing Resources

for Pet Businesses, Veterinary Practices
and Pet-Industry Suppliers/Vendors

We've compiled this list to help you find resources for your marketing efforts. Some of them have special offers for our Wildly Profitable Marketing readers.

Ongoing Success Ideas

WildlyProfitableMarketing.com www.wildlyprofitablemarketing.com
Join us to stay up-to-date on all aspects of marketing, to talk with the authors, and to master your marketing approaches through tools, coaching and other programs that dig deeper into the concepts presented in this guide.

Copywriting, SEO and Content Marketing

PetCopywriter.com www.petcopywriter.com
Pam Foster, Certified SEO Copywriter and Content Marketing Consultant, specializes in web/SEO content, blogs, emails, landing pages, case studies and content marketing planning for the pet industry. Contact Pam for a free initial review of your web content. pam@petcopywriter.com 843-597-6515

Email List Rentals

The List Warehouse www.thelistwarehouse.com Marketing list rentals, consulting and analysis for email, direct mail and more. $50 REBATE COUPON CODE: PETS. Use this code when filling out their online Request Form or calling them about their services. This exclusive coupon for our readers gives you a $50 rebate off your first email list rental.

Email Marketing Systems

The following email marketing services are very similar (with the exception of Pawsitive Perks). Check out each service to see which one feels right for you.

Aweber.com http://aweber.com/?392697

MailYourMarket.com www.mailyourmarket/?affid=petbook

PawsitivePerks.com for pet retailers and farm/feed supply stores. Pawsitive Perks is an automated, customizable email/customer loyalty rewards program that helps pet retailers put their marketing on autopilot. Find out how this "all in one" platform for small pet business owners provides as affordable, turn-key marketing solution that will safely, steadily, and reliably grow their sales. www.PawsitivePerks.com/Pet

Graphic Design: Print and Web

7 Lucky Dogs www.7LuckyDogs.com

Dara Turransky, Graphic and Web Designer Consultant, specializes in corporate identity, web design, retail packaging, and marketing communications. Contact Dara for a free 30-minute consult of your marketing and sales materials, web site or packaging design. dara@7luckydogs.com 425-337-6634

Bonnie Carberry www.bonniecarberry.com

Bonnie has over 20 years of interactive design and marketing, with an emphasis in the veterinary industry. To see samples of her work, please visit her website.

Ericson Mitchell Design www.ericsonmitchell.com

Lynn Ericson and her talented team offer logos, web design, advertising, brochures, trade show and exhibit design. "We apply 20 years of experience in the corporate world to our passion for pets and pet-related businesses. We'd be glad to brainstorm with you for free." lynn@ericsonmitchell.com 207-929-4226

HatchHaus Design / fresh ideas for your brand
www.hatchhaus design.com

Diana Laird, freelance graphic designer, specializes in brand consistency and intelligently designed sales and marketing communications. Contact Diana for $250 off your new logo design (regular $2,500.00). (Mention *Wildly Profitable Marketing for the Pet Industry*.) diana@hatchhausdesign.com 207-318-3274

Hosting Companies

HostGator.com

HostGator is one of the world's top 10 largest web hosting companies with more than 7,000,000 hosted domains. Visit this page to learn more: http://secure.hostgator.com/~affiliat/cgi-bin/affiliates/clickthru.cgi?id=wildlyprofitable

iBest.net LLC, Web Hosting and Development www.ibest.net

Comprehensive Windows or Linux hosting at competitive prices. Save 20% off your initial annual hosting agreement by mentioning Wildly Profitable Marketing for the Pet Industry. Cwo@ibest.net 910-791-8675

Illustration/Pet Portraits

Lynn Ericson Fine Art

Animal illustration and pet portraits are a specialty of Lynn Ericson's. See her samples at her Facebook Fan Page www.facebook.com/lynnericsonfineart.
lynn@ericsonmitchell.com 207-929-4226

Link-Building

LinkVehicle.com www.linkvehicle.com

This SEO advertising company connects advertisers with top-notch publishers to drive generate results and revenue. They provide free consulting to help marketers achieve the results they're looking for. Receive a 15 % discount when you sign up. Use this signup page: http://tinyurl.com/86rlebl
Kyle Hurley, Sales Director 855-281-9304 AIM: Kyle LinkVehicle

Marketing Strategy and Planning

Wildly Profitable Marketing www.wildlyprofitablemarketing.com

C S Wurzberger, Marketing Strategist
No more feeling overwhelmed! Master your marketing and produce profits with a simple-to-follow marketing system. Align with a team that specializes in the pet industry as well as zoos, aquariums, nature centers and their suppliers. We'll roll up our sleeves and work side-by-side with you to assess your current marketing issues, set attainable goals, map out strategies, set up your marketing calendar, timeline and budget. Contact C S at 802-258-8046 or cs@WildlyProfitableMarketing.com and mention this book for a free mini-marketing review.

Mobile App Development (Mobile Apps, Mobile-Friendly Sites)

Idextrus

We build pet mobile applications and mobile-friendly websites. Visit this web page for details: www.idextrus.com/?affid=petbook

PawsitivePerks.com for pet retailers and farm & feed supply stores
The pet industry's first autopilot Customer Loyalty Rewards Card program for independent retailers also offers a customizable pet store mobile app and mobile-website service. Pawsitive Perks sets up everything so all rewards members can quickly access points and rewards on their iPhones (and soon, Androids).
www.PawsitivePerks.com/Pet

PPC (Pay-Per-Click) Advisors/Campaign Managers

SearchGuru.com www.thesearchguru.com/pay-per-click-services.asp
The Search Guru has AdWords Qualified Professionals who are experts with all pay per click services and can help you with your PPC management. Contact The Search Guru to discover how they can help your company. Be sure to mention this book!
Leslie Carruthers, Owner leslie@thesearchguru.com 440-306-2418

Photography (custom)

Nance Trueworthy Photography www.nancetrueworthy.com
Specializing in stock and location photography with a special emphasis on animal photography. Great stock photo images available, including cats, dogs and horses. Call or email with your requests:
nstphoto@gwi.net 207-774-6181

Leslie Wagner Photo www.lesliewagnerphoto.com/dogs.html
What makes a pet irresistible in photography? It's the facial expression, body language and setting. Leslie integrates these elements to tell a story - either of a product, a lifestyle, a company or a beloved family pet. An experienced pet wrangler, she understands the importance of creating the proper environment, keeping the models relaxed, focused, comfortable, and enjoying themselves so they can

give you their best work.
leslie@lesliewagnerphoto.com 207-272-3498

Public Relations Management

Public Relations/Marketing Communications
www.ConstantGroup.com
Cathy Levendoski, president of Constant Communications, has 20 years of experience in marketing and public relations, specializing in media relations for vendors in the veterinary industry. Contact Cathy for a review of your current PR plans.
clevendoski@constantgroup.com 314-725-2594

Rembrandt Communications, LLC www.rembrandtwrites.com
Increase sales, awareness and credibility within weeks with B2B Search Engine Optimization, public relations. Mention "WildlyProfitable" on our online contact-form and receive a free, initial consultation.
Melanie@rembrandtwrites.com 310-406-5105

PR Distribution

Pet PR Distribution
PetPR.com www.petpr.com

OnlinePRMedia.com

PR.com

PRNewswire.com

PRWeb.com

QR Code Generator

Immediatag http://immediatag.com
A mobile tagging platform that makes it easy to engage and inform visitors through their mobile devices. Compatible with QR codes and other popular bridge technologies. A variety of affordable month-to-month plans available. Visit our website to sign up for a free 30-day trial today!

Social Media Marketing

Black Dog Studios www.BlackDogDev.com
An integrated web design and development firm focused on goal-oriented, result driven development. We build sites that perform. Contact Mike Linville for a FREE 30-minute strategy session. m.linville@blackdogdev.com 916-608-2151

Emily Susan 007 www.emilysusan007.com
Helping independent business owners profit from their social media. Your personal agent for social media success. Contact Emily at Emily@EmilySusan007.com

Success Coaching for Pet Businesses

TheGreenUpGirl.com www.TheGreenUpGirl.com
Green your business from the inside out: audit, supply chain, waste reduction and cost savings.

Veterinary Reminders

Creative Marketing Solutions www.creativecms.com/
The Total Reminder Solution from Creative Marketing Solutions offers email and text reminders, in addition to high-quality, custom postal reminders. Call today, mention Wildly Profitable Marketing, and receive a free custom reminder card, branded for your practice, plus a free month of unlimited email and text reminders. info@cmsintouch.com 800-540-6910

Video Production

Catama Productions www.catama.net

Catama serves clients with creative, engaging video content for broadcast, corporate video communications and web/new media missions. We have many years of experience in the pet/veterinary related industry. Contact us to discuss your video project and receive a free consultation. info@catama.net 207-874-4974

Website Development (Custom)

Black Dog Studios www.BlackDogDev.com

An integrated web design and development firm focused on goal-oriented, result driven development. We build sites that perform. Contact Mike Linville for a FREE 30-minute strategy session. m.linville@blackdogdev.com 916-608-2151

Idextrus.com

We build pet Internet solutions that work, and we look forward to meeting you!

Get a free 30-minute consultation on your existing web presence (structural and functional audit) as well as ideas to make the web do more for you. Visit this web page for details: www.idextrus.com/?affid=petbook

Image Works www.imagewks.com

We have the experience and resources to deliver your project and results on-time, on-budget. Drupal 7, WordPress, .Net and App design and development. Clients have included Fortune 500 corporations, innovative non-profits and small businesses since. Interactive media marketing since 1977! Mention this book and ask about our special offer of the week.

dana@imagewks.com or misty@imagewks.com 800.32IMAGE (800.324.6243)

Website Development Systems (Template Based)

BigCommerce.com

HostGator.com

Web123.com

Weebly.com

WordPress.com

Website System Specifically for Veterinarians

WebDVM4 (LifeLearn)
Market your veterinary practice and enhance compliance through educational and informative websites that make it easy to manage new content, social media and more.
Save $50 off of the license fee for a new WebDVM4 account (upgrades not eligible). Visit http://marketing.lifelearn.com/acton/media/1997/learn-more-about-webdvm4 to take advantage of this offer.

Web Analytics

Your own host's traffic logs

Analytics.Admob.com

Google Analytics http://www.google.com/analytics/

QUICK ORDER FORM

Wildly Profitable Marketing for the Pet Industry

Powerful pointers for your pet business,
veterinary practice or pet-industry supply company

E-mail orders: info@PawzoolaPublishing.com

Postal orders: Please send this form and a check to:
Pawzoola Publishing,
a division of A Trip to the Zoo.com
P.O. Box 1779
Wilmington, VT 05363
www.PawzoolaPublishing.com

Please send me the following number of copies of this book: _____

Please contact me to discuss:

☐ Speaking/Seminars on Profitable Marketing Strategies
or Web Marketing Topics
☐ Consulting/Evaluating My Current Site
☐ Developing a Sustainability and/or PR Marketing Plan for My Business

Name: _____

Address: _____

City: _____ State: _____ ZIP: _____

Telephone: _____

E-mail Address: _____

*Do you wish to be added to our e-mail list to receive website success tips and
announcements?*

Yes ☐   No ☐

Pricing: Please send for each book:
$16.95 List Price
$5 Shipping/Handling
Vermont Sales Tax: 6%
$22.97 Total Remittance in the USA.
Please e-mail us for International pricing.

Thank you!